"*When It's Never About You* is no ordinary self-help book, but rather an insightful guide using a time honored theory (Bowen) to assist the reader into becoming more of a self, finding their true voice, and authoring their preferred story for living. The author uses both her personal journey of self-discovery and clinical examples to highlight new ways of "growing oneself;" shedding light on ways of thinking and acting that can transform functioning in relationships. Every personal journey needs a map to traverse the territory. Anyone who reads the concepts and vignettes provided by Dr. Ilene will be greatly rewarded to find themselves standing on more solid ground with their family, their relationships and their sense of self. People with curiosity about their functioning in all kinds of relationships will profit from the wisdom proffered in this reader-friendly book."

~ Jim Rudes, Ph.D, LMFT, LCSW,
Associate Professor Barry University

"In her book *When It's Never About You,* Dr. Ilene offers a wonderful, accessible and practical guide for anyone who is looking to take charge of their life, and shed the guilt and exhaustion of pleasing and looking for others' approval. As a family therapist, she gives readers an understanding into family systems and how to view your own role in your family and intimate relationships. This insight will give readers an opportunity to implement real change that will make relationships more enriching, and allow others to take responsibility for themselves."

~ Olivia Schlapfer Colmer, Ph.D., LMFT

"Having spent 32 out of my 33 years stuck in a cycle of constant people pleasing, I can't begin to express how it felt to learn, through this *When It's Never About You*, that I was not alone in how I lived and that there were indeed ways to stay out of the people-pleasing zone. Dr. Ilene's candid and honest examples of how she, too, was stuck in the debilitating cycle of pleasing were refreshing, and how she found her way out of that tangled web was extremely inspiring. This is a self-help book that feels more like a personal support group, one where a brilliant writer and psychotherapist reminds you that you're not alone, and teaches you how to live a self-full life, without guilt, and with total confidence."

~ MICHELLE DEMPSEY, Former people-pleaser

"Dr. Ilene's book is a great read for those who are constantly challenged with the need to please others. I have no doubt that it will allow readers to gain a new perspective and acquire some very useful tips on becoming fulfilled without the need to please others."

~ THALIA RYDZ, LCSW

"In life, many of us get caught in wanting to be the person for everyone else; our need to help, make it easier on someone, etc. Dr. Ilene shows us how to fulfill this need while still being a healthy FULL person in this easy to read guide. My colleague reminded me that life must be "SELF-FULL" to be SELF-Fufilled!"

~ DR. EDRICA D. RICHARDSON, LMFT

When It's *Never* About You

The People-Pleaser's Guide to
Reclaiming Your Health, Happiness
and Personal Freedom

ILENE S.COHEN, Ph.D.

HARTE & CO PUBLISHING • MIAMI FLORIDA

When It's Never *About You*

by Ilene S. Cohen, Ph.D.

© 2017 Ilene S. Cohen, Ph.D.

www.doctorilene.com

Published by Harte & Co Publishing

Copywriter: Peter Bowerman

Proofreader: Denise Fournier

Book design: Chris Molé

ISBN: 978-0-9993115-0-9

First Edition

Printed in the United States of America

DEDICATION

To my family, without whom
I wouldn't be the person I am today.
We are forever interconnected,
and I wouldn't have it any other way.

SELF LOVE

Once when I was running,
from all that haunted me;
to the dark I was succumbing-
to what hurt unbearably.

Searching for the one thing,
that would set my sad soul free.

In time I stumbled upon it,
an inner calm and peace;
and now I am beginning,
to see and to believe,
in who I am becoming-
and all I've yet to be.

~ LANG LEAV

CONTENTS

PREFACE

You have inherited a lifetime of tribulation. Everybody has inherited it. Take it over, make the most of it and when you have decided you know the right way, do the best you can with it.

~ Murray Bowen

IN MY PHILOSOPHY OF LIFE, things don't just happen without rhyme or reason. We don't aimlessly walk around making choices with no purpose, meaning, or significance to our lives. I say this because I believe you picked up this book for a reason—perhaps because you need a change in your life. Many choices we make, including the books we decide to read, shape the way we think and lead us to make meaningful changes in our lives. All these meaningful changes start with awareness. This makes it important for us to read and educate ourselves in ways that can help us with whatever we might be going through at a particular point in life, bringing more awareness to that situation. My purpose for writing this book is to help you build a strong sense of self, agency, and competency—something I call *self-full living*. If you find yourself in a people-pleasing pattern in your relationships, you may be experiencing a loss of self, a loss of awareness of your internal world. You may constantly find yourself completely neglecting what you want—or not even knowing what you want in the first place—in order to do what you believe someone else wants.

I get it. I created the word *self-full* while trying to find a healthy balance between being selfless and selfish in my own life. Born into difficult family circumstances, I did everything possible to cope. My efforts to be helpful, which ultimately involved conforming to everyone's expectations, weren't very helpful at all. However, I kept doing the same behaviors, even when they weren't working. As much as I wanted to be more aware of myself, I found that over time, my mission to build myself up was thwarted by my resistance to being viewed as selfish. My experiences make it easy for me to understand that it's hard to adopt the open-mindedness it takes to become truly self-full, perfectly balanced between selfishness and selflessness. So, let me be the first to commend you for taking the initial step toward self-full living.

Creating a Sense of Self Within Your Relationships

I want you to reflect a moment on the following question: What is the force that holds the solar system together? As you bring yourself back to 5th grade science, you may recall that the answer is gravity. Gravity is the powerful force that keeps our universe together. It helped form our solar system, the planets, and the stars. It's what holds the planets in orbit around the sun, and moons in orbit around the planets. If there were no gravitational force on planets, people would float off into the sky. So it's safe to say that gravity plays a significant role in our survival.

If you only see the solar system as planets out in space acting on their own without influence, you're likely to miss the bigger picture: that each planet works as part of a greater system, in which everything influences everything else. This same idea applies to viewing an individual as a single entity with no influence from the outside world, failing to see that each person is part of a system of relationships that influence each other. Dr. Murray Bowen, whose ideas make up Family Systems Theory, a common approach to family therapy, proposed that people should not be understood in isolation from one another, but rather as a part of the emotional unit of their families of origin. Seeing the family as an emotional unit suggests that what one family member does will affect the other members of that family system. A family isn't just a bunch of separate people walking around freely; the gravitational pull influencing family members is the emotional connection they have to one another.

We live in a culture that sees problems as residing within individuals. We tend to see people out of context, as if they were isolated from their surroundings. Our planets could not possibly exist without gravity allowing them to orbit, and so it is with humans. We do not exist without our relationships. Real change begins with the awareness that we create our sense of self within our relationships, not apart from them. This book is designed to support you in becoming self-aware in the context of your relationships and honoring that problems do not reside within individuals, but in the interconnections with others. I wrote it to show how the gravity that pulls us all together connects us in important ways, ultimately making us who we are. This book will assist you in understanding this process more deeply so that you can put these lessons into action in your own life. My hope is that what you read will inspire you to become more aware of the part you play in your relationship systems, and that this will lead you to explore new possibilities for yourself and your emotional unit.

Selfless Narrative

Throughout this book, I'll be sharing my personal narrative, along with a few of my clients' stories. But what's most important is *your* story. The story you feel has been written for you by other people. The story that doesn't fit with your true nature, because it's overly focused on others. Your life experiences may have led you to believe that you must spend your life saying yes to everyone. This selfless narrative will convince you that you're only as good as the good you do for others. This story must be re-written—and you must be the author of that rewrite! No matter your age, circumstance, race, sex, or religion, now is the time to stop the cycle of people-pleasing. Living to please others is draining, lonely, and damaging to your health. If you've started to discover this in your own life, you might be thinking, How do I even begin to change it? Well, I've got good news. By picking up this book, you've already begun the change process. You've started to re-write your narrative by realizing that something needs to be different in your life. As with most significant life changes, it's up to you to create that difference. You, more than anyone else, deserve to be the author of your own story. So, let's start writing it!

About Me

Before we go any further, allow me to introduce myself. My name is Ilene Strauss Cohen, but many people refer to me as Doctor Ilene. I hold a Ph.D. in Marriage and Family Therapy, and I work with clients who have no *sense of self*—essentially, people who have a hard time knowing where they end and other people begin. These people are prone to pleasing behaviors, and they often suffer because of it. Using my knowledge—both personal and professional—about what it's like to live this way, I've dedicated myself to helping people-pleasers live differently.

Do you have a tough time saying no? Do you struggle with thinking you might be letting people down? Have you found yourself wishing you could make yourself a priority but unsure how to do it? If so, I feel your frustration. I know how hard it can be to live your life that way, never feeling good enough, constantly feeding an impulse to please, finding it hard to say no to others and yes to your needs. Life isn't just complex, it's straight up paralyzing at times—particularly when you're trying to be what everyone else expects you to be. But you're likely to find that even if you comply with everyone's wishes and whims, they still won't be happy. And, of course, you won't be either! Welcome to the paradox of relationships; welcome to the deception of people-pleasing.

Growing up, I discovered that I had a certain automatic way of dealing with stress, which I thought helped guide me through some tough times. As challenging as things sometimes were, I continued to engage in the same behavior patterns, thinking I would get the outcome I wanted. My most difficult moment came when my grandfather died. Not only did I lose someone very close to me, but his passing set off a series of events that changed my life forever. After his death, I was left in charge of handling his estate, something I wasn't mentally prepared to take on at 24 years old. I decided that the best way to handle the challenge of becoming an overnight executor of a complicated estate was to accommodate my family members' every wish. This strategy ultimately backfired on me, like this way of thinking always had. I found myself consumed with worry about everyone else's well-being and happiness, never taking into account my own.

I believed that by constantly aiming to please others, I

was making everyone—including myself—happy. As time went on, I started to realize that this strategy wasn't working very well at all. As my urge to please became overwhelming, my drive to become my own self grew stronger. I had spent my life constantly giving in and doing things for other people, negotiating things that should have been non-negotiable in my relationships. Living selflessly affected me in many aspects of my life. I wasn't able to say no. I felt guilty all the time. I didn't do things for myself. I let go of my own dreams. Eventually, I found myself empty, alone, and endlessly exhausted. My relationships became one-sided; they seemed to work fine for everyone else in my life, but they were no longer working for me. I started to lose myself in my relationships with others and thought that if only I could do a little bit more, I'd feel better about myself. But this didn't work. In fact, it had the opposite effect.

For years, I tried to find myself by losing myself in my relationships with others. Naturally, it didn't work. I wound up feeling alone and lost, at a complete standstill in my life. Although I knew the way I was living wasn't working, I still had a strong urge to do everything that was asked of me. I didn't know how to stop it, and parts of me didn't want to. The truth is, I was addicted to people-pleasing—or, at least, it felt like I was. Doing what others wanted and expected from me made me feel euphoric at first; but after the high wore off, I realized I wasn't helping anyone. I was only making things worse. This led me to start resenting the people who continued to make the same mistakes in their lives, no matter how hard I tried to help them. I thought, if only I can get better at helping them, they'll finally make better choices, and I won't need to do so much for them anymore.

My grandfather's passing was the singular life-altering moment that pushed me out of this state of being, allowing me to focus on myself. It left me with no choice but to toughen up and grow a stronger backbone. I knew that if I didn't, everyone in my life would suffer. I had no time to accomplish my own goals and aspirations, and no energy to do so either. My grandfather's death opened up the opportunity for me to realize that I had no boundaries in my relationships. My family and friends had become so dependent on me to do so much for them that I couldn't keep my head above water. At first, I wrongly thought that if other people in my life would just be less demanding, or if I could just cut out the difficult people, then my life would be easier and I could be the person I wanted to be. But what I didn't realize is that I was drowning in a pool that I—and no one else—had filled with water.

Constantly falling into the trap of people-pleasing, I eventually started to wonder if I'd ever get around to accomplishing my own goals. Would I ever find a way to make others feel happy and appreciated while also tending to my own wants and needs? Exploring this question marked the first step of my journey.

Through my own process of self-discovery, I went from being a shy girl with little nerve to a self-reliant, self-confident woman with plenty of moxie. When I finally got sick and tired of trying to be everyone's hero, I changed my mindset and started to champion my own cause. I turned the negative effects of my grandfather's passing into motivation for honoring his legacy appropriately. This fueled my ever-changing process of growth. Through this book, I can show you how to change your perceptions, behaviors, and relationships so you can design a fulfilling life for yourself. When viewed and understood through different lenses, life can be amazing. But you won't know how amazing it can be if you have no direction or goals for yourself. I changed my response to people by carefully examining every situation that presented me with the choice to please others, take blame, or act more for self. This process taught me how to live self-fully. Now I'm here to help you make similar discoveries in your own life. Are you ready to take the journey with me?

Self-Full Living Guide

I've created this guide after reading many books about many subjects. My brain is the kind that seeks to know everything about everything: psychology, neurology, world religions, finances, biology, history, and the list goes on. I'm revealing my inner nerd to make the point that reading has aided me in obtaining information, understanding concepts and theories, and indulging in the universe's many complexities. However, much of the information that guides my life and work has been derived from Bowen's Family Systems Theory. I have read extensively, researched, and attended trainings in order to become well educated in this specific theory. I did this not only because it has been instrumental in helping my clients live more fulfilling lives, but also because it has changed my own life.

As valuable as education is, the knowledge contained in books is only meaningful if it's applied through mindful and purposeful action. My true knowledge developed when I tried the ideas on for size in my own life and found tremendous value in doing so. I want the same for you. I hope you can use this book as a guide for gaining the strength to live the life you've always known you deserve. I wrote this book in such a way that the ideas can easily be applied to anyone's situation. Follow the guide in whatever way makes sense and feels right to you. Make decisions based on what feels like a good fit for your circumstances.

If you read my blog, you know I'm all about challenging commonly held beliefs. Ideas and beliefs are very powerful, because most of us go around treating them as facts and truths. We let them dictate how we live our lives. People who go through life people-pleasing don't challenge common beliefs about what people *should* do or how they *ought to* behave; instead, they take them on as true. As you read this book, I want you to open your mind and start challenging the beliefs and ideas that got you into the people-pleasing position. I especially want you to challenge those ideas that don't match with your experiences. Once you do that, you'll have more freedom of choice in your life. I give you permission to challenge some of the advice I offer here as well. Keep only what fits for you and what you think can help you start making yourself a priority. Let go of what doesn't work for you. This book is only a map to guide you; where the journey leads is totally up to you.

I wrote each chapter with the intention to explain new concepts and offer specific ways to apply those concepts through simple activities included at the end of each chapter. You'll likely find it most helpful to concentrate on one chapter at a time, applying each activity to your life for as long as you believe it's creating meaningful changes. In traditional therapy, you see your therapist once a week and use the time between sessions to apply any new skills you've learned. I wrote this guide with that process in mind. What's important is that you be intentional about applying the concepts without feeling constrained by time. Learning new behaviors takes a lot of patience, persistence and time. There's no need to rush.

INTRODUCTION

When you are sorrowful look again in your heart, and you shall see that in truth you are weeping for that which has been your delight.

~ KAHLIL GIBRAN

I SAT BY THE SIDE OF HIS BED and held his cold hand tightly. I knew he didn't have long. All I wanted was to be there with him, and for him, during his final days. They say that in the final moments of life, we can hear everything around us, even if we aren't conscious. Despite believing that, I didn't know what to say to him. Words escaped me, and anything I could think of seemed trivial under the circumstances. It was especially uncomfortable to say anything while the hospice nurses scurried around trying to make him comfortable. I kept hoping he would open his eyes again, that the doctors had made some kind of mistake and he would wake up as if nothing had happened. I wondered who I would be without him, and I feared that everything and everyone would fall apart in his absence.

As I sat beside him in those final moments, I remembered the rabbi saying that when death is near, we should let him know it's okay for him to leave us. When the nurses left the room, I whispered in his ear, "Grandpa, I love you. It's okay. You can leave us now." I said those words, but I didn't mean them. The "I love you" part was real, but the rest felt like a lie. I knew I was being selfish, but I didn't know how I was supposed to function without him. Saying goodbye was just too difficult. There was so much I wanted to say out loud—so much I was feeling inside—but I knew I wasn't supposed to vocalize it.

So, I held his hand and sat silently by his side while he rested in his bed. All he could say at the end was, "Bring me home." He had spent many days and nights in that room, which looked like it hadn't been re-decorated since the 1950s. The only updated part of it was the picture of him and me in a plain gold frame that sat on his nightstand.

We all know that people don't live forever and that we'll likely lose a loved one at some point in our lives. But it's still always a shock when it happens. When someone you love is being taken from you, there's no ignoring the facts; they smack you hard in the face, forcing you to come to terms with mortality. This was how it was for me. With every day that passed, I lost my beloved grandfather a little bit more. There was nothing I could do about it.

I lost him forever on October 3, 2008. When it happened, I knew that life would never be the same. But I had no idea just how much my reality would change. At 24 years old, in the first semester of my doctoral program, I had the world in the palm of my hand. But suddenly, it wasn't about me anymore. It's almost as if my grandfather and I both lost our lives that day. He had been the one everyone in our family would always turn to, and I had spent my lifetime aiming to please others. So, when he left us, I stepped into his role completely and started to function for everyone in my family. It was part of our unique way of responding to a crisis. One person was knighted to take over for the family, to be the leader. At the time, it was my own instinctive reaction to be that person. I truly believed it was my only option.

After the coroner left, I took the picture of my grandfather and me from the nightstand. Looking at it, I remembered our time together and all of the lessons I learned from him. My grandfather was a selfless man, who always put others' needs before his own. I used to think that was a good thing; but as it turns out, doing everything for everyone made things worse for the people he emotionally supported. The value of enough seemed to be lost on our family, and excessively asking for help was the status quo. They became focused on getting what they wanted from others and failed to take responsibility for their own behaviors. It was hard for them to delay gratification and work hard, which made it difficult for them to accomplish their life goals.

When people have everything done for them, they don't have to deal with the consequences of their decisions. They don't learn from their mistakes. They rarely self-reflect and don't often admit to the role they play in creating their problems. I found myself at my grandfather's funeral surrounded by people who had never learned to take responsibility for their actions. I truly believed I had to hold these people together by taking on my grandfather's role of over-functioning, but I didn't know how to hold on to myself in the process.

At 24 years old, I said goodbye to my life and took over my grandfather's role: living to take care of everyone else. That proved to be a huge mistake. I knew my life would change in important ways, but at the time I had no idea what kinds of twists and turns that would include. I hated twists and turns. I couldn't even ride a rollercoaster or go on a playground swing without getting nauseous. My life was about calmness and relaxation; I tried to avoid drama and conflict, aiming to keep the peace in my relationships as much as possible. I lost myself in trying to find ways to keep everyone else happy.

There was no way I could have prepared for the way the dynamics in all my close relationships changed after my grandfather died, and I certainly wasn't ready to bury my old life along with burying him. I stood on the stage next to my grandfather's coffin completely numb, saying what I had to say in front of everyone. Once I finished speaking, I walked away from the microphone and away from the life I had known, stepping into a new world of coldness and cluelessness—a world that would prove to be uninhabitable for the people-pleaser I had become.

When I first entered this new life, I was completely blind. But over time, I came to see that there are some things in life we have to learn, whether we like it or not. There are people we must learn to let go of and situations we must learn to accept. When you've lost a loved one, there's nothing anyone can do to bring the person back; there's nothing anyone can say to take the pain away. Grief can make one hour feel like ten. But I learned, through my own process, that it's important to feel what you're feeling no matter how painful it is. As Golda Meir, fourth elected Prime Minister of Israel, said, "Those who do not know how to weep with their whole hearts don't know how to laugh either." After my grandfather passed, I became so attuned with how everyone else felt about losing him that I made no time to grieve my loss, too. It took years of tending to others' emotions for me to finally give myself permission to grieve. I wasn't living for myself, and I was blaming others for it. It was my grandfather's fault, I thought, for not setting the proper ground rules, and my family was to blame for being unappreciative and self-involved. What I finally came to understand is that, in fact, I was the one who placed those shackles on my hands and feet. And only I could set myself free.

Throughout this book, I'll share many examples of the opportunities life gives you to grow. In my case, having a grandfather who handled everything played a role in stunting the growth of everyone in my family unit. Our culture is centered on a belief that people who are selfless are doing the right thing. Insinuating that people who give all of themselves are immune to struggle and difficulty. I understand this perspective completely and had lived with that perspective for many years. But the truth is, *all* people, regardless of how much they give, have problems. At times in my life, I have found myself depressed, alone, and overwhelmed. I've felt guilty about experiencing negative emotions. I've found a real limit to the cultural notion that always giving buys happiness; it simply doesn't fit with my experience. I hope, this book, demonstrates that always doing for others at your own expense doesn't automatically translate to having a life of value. It certainly doesn't fix your problems. I'll tell you about how some of the mistakes I made in handling my circumstances changed my understanding of life and the way I live it.

For the longest time, I tried to make everyone else happy while forgetting about myself. It was a tireless, thankless, fruitless effort that always left me falling on my face. I knew that something desperately needed to change; I needed to strike a workable balance between selfishness and selflessness, because what I was doing wasn't working. But I had no idea what to do differently or how to go about doing it. That's when the idea of self-fullness came to me. I realized I could strike a healthy balance that would allow me to stay connected and kind to others in a way that also allowed me to prioritize my own needs. I realized that it's possible for me to get along with my family members and keep things in harmony without stuffing down my feelings or totally cutting them out of my life. This awareness saved my relationships. It saved my life. Learning that my family was an emotional unit and that all our actions influence each other opened my eyes to see that if I changed, so would they. Once I discovered the possibility of self-fullness, I set out to start living a self-full life. Sounds simple enough, right? Think again.

When It's
Never About You

CHAPTER I

. . .

Awareness of Self

*You cannot solve a problem from the same consciousness
that created it. You must learn to see the world anew.*

~ ALBERT EINSTEIN

FOR MANY YEARS, Emma didn't live her life the way she truly wanted to; and even though she had some awareness of this, she never wanted to admit it to herself. The road she was taking wasn't leading anywhere, but she convinced herself that one day, when her family issues disappeared, everything would perfectly align. One day she would make her dream of becoming a nurse come true.

When she came to therapy she was well aware of everything she thought was holding her back: nonexistent family support; urgent family matters, excessive preoccupation with helping others; lack of this, that, or the other. The laundry list of seemingly logical reasons why she couldn't possibly grow was endless. However, Emma was fixed on the idea that she was caring for her family by always doing what they asked of her. What she didn't understand was that by hyper-focusing on others, she was missing out on a huge opportunity for growth. She believed that if only her family members would start taking care of their responsibilities or doing things right the first time, she could finally move on with her life. However, all this did was cause her to live in ways that didn't align with her potential. Emma wasn't really living her life; she was simply going through the motions.

Going through life people-pleasing is kind of like sleep-walking; you're disconnected from your true self. For many years, Emma was asleep, stuck in a never-ending dream in which she was a servant trying to please others and satisfy their demands of her. After years of failing to sign up for nursing school, she finally decided to wake up and do something for herself. That's when her real growth began. It was natural for Emma to believe that if other people would only change, then she would finally be able to reach her goals. After getting tired of waiting, she realized that fulfilling her dreams started with learning to take responsibility for herself. Emma was able to do this by becoming aware of the part she played in her family system. She developed a greater awareness of herself within her relationships and owned up to what was really motivating her actions. Once she created this shift in her mindset, she was able to make meaningful changes.

People-pleasers tend to believe that doing things for other people—be they family members, friends, or co-workers—is a requirement for being a good, nice, and responsible person. They think that by acting in pleasing ways, they'll somehow be immune to criticism, hurt, or rejection. They'll avoid confrontation at all costs in order to stuff down the pain and discomfort that comes with disagreeing with someone or having to deal with their negative reactions. Living this way keeps them from learning valuable lessons. It makes it harder for them to navigate challenges and appropriately manage things like conflict, unpleasant emotions, loss, and disappointment. It's easy for people-pleasers to give others control of their lives, only to later wonder why they're always dissatisfied, depleted, and surrounded by demanding people.

Emma's need to please always felt like a compulsion; it left her unable to control her own life. Everything she did was dictated by her need to make other people happy, and her worth depended on others' approval. Emma didn't feel like she had control of her emotions, decisions, or self. Other people had all the say, which she experienced as a very uncomfortable way to live. When you have the desire to please, your self-worth is tangled up with how much you do for others and how good you are at pleasing them. This makes it hard to change, because the thought of doing things differently invites fear of how other people will react. You don't connect with your authentic self, because it's too anxiety-provoking to even think of acting in ways that may displease someone else. The only way out of this dilemma is to start becoming aware of your own internal world, recognizing that the only person you can change is yourself. At first, changing can feel uncomfortable and impossible. Even if your old behaviors haven't been working, you'll naturally fall back into familiar patterns of pleasing or blaming. If Emma could only change her perspective and notice that her instinctive reactions were keeping her family members from becoming more responsible, she'd finally be able to start living her own life.

It's Not Selfish; It's Self-Full

If you're anything like Emma, you've probably been believing that it's selfish to consider your needs first. Taking your focus off other people and placing it on yourself is commonly viewed as a selfish thing to do. Realizing that this isn't the case can be life-changing. Once Emma made some necessary adjustments in her life, she started to become more attuned to her own needs. She was able to change her perspective by shifting her idea of what it means to be a good, responsible, and helpful person. Part of Emma's change process came with the realization that if she didn't start valuing herself, her relationships would suffer. Although it might seem counterintuitive, prioritizing your needs and gaining a strong sense of self is actually *better* for your relationships, because it serves to strengthen them. It's for this reason that connecting with yourself isn't selfish; it's *self-full*. It means being in relationships without losing yourself or avoiding uncomfortable issues. It means not impulsively doing for others what they can learn to do for themselves. It means not taking personally other people's reactive responses or blaming yourself when others get upset. It means considering yourself within the context of your relationships instead of focusing only on what you can do for someone else. Ultimately, self-fullness means knowing that you are only responsible for yourself.

If you can't be clear about what you want and express it to the people you're in relationship with, you—and those relationships—will suffer. That's because the ingredients for healthy human connection (authenticity, honesty, intimacy, etc.) will be lost. You won't be able to speak up when you're angry, hurt, or feel violated, because you'll be too worried about preserving your anxiety and avoiding others' reactions. This is normal; we all want other people to approve of and like us. It's programmed into each and every one of us. However, you're bound to start resenting other people if you're only concerned with what they think of you. Contrary to what some believe, speaking up is an important aspect of any relationship; avoiding it robs you of meaningful connection.

When you aren't acting for self, you lose your identity, agency, and competency. You lose yourself, getting caught up in the urge to please others. This makes you susceptible to things like perfectionism, anxiety, and addiction. All of this because you're living as the person you think you should be for society, family, friends, co-workers, and even strangers. You're left adrift because you've abandoned your inner voice, authenticity, and self. As a result, you start seeking fulfillment outside yourself. You end up dependent, relying on others' opinions of you to give you worth. Only after gaining confidence in yourself and taking the initiative to satisfy your needs can you begin to lead a more self-full life.

The empowering aspect of living more self-fully is taking the first step: becoming self-aware. After that it's a matter of consistently changing your behaviors to match your awareness of self. Once you've generated some momentum, the process of changing your behaviors will get easier, becoming more natural over time. If you let it, your fear will keep you paralyzed, holding you prisoner in a life that isn't yours. Instead of waiting for something or someone else to allow you to be self-full, give yourself permission to live a more balanced life. Discover what you want in this world, and then use this guide to help you go out and get it. When you have long term goals and a strong desire to change, you're motivated to do what's necessary. With an increase in purpose, your gravitational pull moves you in the direction of autonomy, and you start to increase your personal boundaries within your relationships.

When we face challenges in life, some of us function well, some muddle through, and some don't do well at all. There are some people who have a hard time functioning adaptively even under normal circumstances, so when they're faced with a challenge, they fall apart. Most of us find a way to cope with life's challenges without engaging in much deep thought; we simply keep doing what we normally do, even if it isn't working. Instead of solving our challenges, we maintain them; we don't make them worse, but we don't make them any better either. That's because we usually see ourselves as being pretty reasonable. We don't look closely at ourselves and instead think about the ways that certain people or circumstances in our lives need to change in order for our challenges to be resolved. We believe that if only we could make other people see things the way we do, everything would be okay. These thoughts and actions usually keep our anxiety at bay for a little while, but when another challenge comes our way, we're anxious once again. It might seem easier to live this way, because we don't have to take responsibility for the ways that we maintain and perpetuate our challenges. We think that taking responsibility means taking the blame; and since it makes us anxious to feel blamed, we aim to reduce our anxiety by placing the blame elsewhere. But the truth is, this doesn't really solve anything. So, what if we could take responsibility for our challenges and actions without taking blame? And what if we could do this by being self-aware when challenges happen?

As I said before, many of us seek to blame others when things don't go according to plan. We think, "If I don't feel happy, other people must be the reason for it." Some of us, on the other hand, have a tendency to always find fault in ourselves. We think, "I'm to blame for everything that goes wrong in my life. If only I could avoid making so many mistakes, I could be free to live a better life." Whether we blame others or blame ourselves, this rigid way of looking at situations doesn't bring lasting change. Each time we face a new challenge, we instinctively seek to place blame somewhere, instigating a cycle of disappointment. We may become resentful of people, blaming them for disappointing us and then cutting them out of our lives as if they were trash to be thrown away.

Whether we see the fault in others or in ourselves, we're missing the bigger picture: relationships are systems, and each person in a relationship deeply influences the other's capacity for emotional flexibility. Lasting growth begins with learning to observe ourselves in our relationships, being aware that problems do not reside within individuals, but rather in the interconnections between them. When we see our relationships this way, our goal becomes to understand how we may be contributing to our challenges in the ways we interact with others when issues arise. It can lead us to take personal responsibility of our own lives and stop playing the blame game. It isn't easy to think this way, but once we can manage it, we gradually begin to transform our lives, even in the most challenging of circumstances. As we become more aware of the effect we have on others, our sense of self and integrity grows. Seeing the role we play in our relationship patterns opens us up to greater honesty, humility, and wellbeing—not only for ourselves, but for the people we're in relationship with also. So how do you undo unhelpful behaviors that may be contributing to your challenges? First, you change the way you think.

Changing Your Mindset

Our mindset contains our ideas, beliefs, and views about life. It is shaped by our previous experiences of the world along with ideas passed down from generations before. The perceptions we form from our past influence our experiences in the present and future, thereby creating our reality. As psychotherapist Michael Kerr, MD said, "The past does not necessarily cause the issues we face in the present; rather, the recreation of a problem that was shaped in the past creates a problem in the present." In other words, situations have a way of repeating themselves if certain patterns aren't interrupted. This is why changing our mindset is so crucial whenever we find ourselves repeating problematic patterns. As we change our mindset, becoming more self-aware, we go from being hyper-focused on others to more self-focused. Once we become aware of the fact that hyper-focusing on others leads to problems in our relationships, we can start focusing on ourselves and bring about more meaningful changes.

My client Emma's mindset had been molded by the types of problems her family experienced over several generations. In each generation, a family member took on the role of helping and functioning for others in the family. When things went wrong, it was up to this person to take care of everything. Once Emma could see that she'd inherited this role, she was able to make a shift. She realized that this wasn't a life sentence, and staying in the role wouldn't be useful for anyone—especially her. At last, she was able to start focusing on her own needs. How adaptable you are in shifting your focus from other people to yourself depends on how you view things. Once you become more self-aware of your automatic nature, like Emma did, ask yourself: "What can I do to understand and deal with the problems I see in others? If I'm playing some small part, can I alter that by changing what I'm thinking or doing?"

Family Systems Theory takes a long-term approach to looking at family systems, offering a different view of the role each family member plays. When you begin to change your mindset, others will adjust their mindsets as well. As a consequence of this, they'll start relating to you and other people in their lives differently. A major strength of Family Systems Theory is that it helps us see there aren't angels or demons in families. Once you see the family as an emotional system, automatically regulating the behaviors of its members, the hurtful behaviors of others become less personal. Awareness of the automatic and reactive nature of our relationship systems allows us to interrupt and challenge old patterns and take more responsibility for our ways of relating to others. Developing a self-full mindset also involves challenging old beliefs—specifically those you've derived from your past experiences that dictate what it means to be a good, responsible, and competent person. Becoming self-full means abandoning the belief that you need to put other people's needs before your own in order to have peaceful relationships.

One of the most important things to have in life is a clear and rational mind; one that belongs to you and isn't controlled or heavily influenced by fads and outside opinions. A life without a solid mind will leave you lost, reactive, and unfulfilled. For many people, achieving this type of mindset is the most challenging part of becoming self-full, because it's an ever-evolving process.

We have little to no control over the things that happen to us in our day-to-day lives. We can't control the families we're born into or what previous generations did before us. But we do have control over how we want to feel and respond to our life circumstances. In deeply anxious or upsetting situations, it's easy to feel out of control. Sometimes it's easier for us to let our emotions override our logical thoughts. It takes real effort for us to gain control over the reactions that tend to follow those overriding emotions. Understanding and accepting that you can develop control over your responses and choices is an important step in your growth process.

The minute you can see your part in the process of your relationships and take ownership of it, you can take control of your own life. Having this sense of control is incredibly empowering. When you consistently hand over control to other people or external circumstances, you aren't living for self. You're waiting for the outside world and the people in it to dictate how you feel about your life. The biggest problem with focusing on others and giving them control is that it leaves you unaware of what you can change about yourself and how you can grow.

Although you can't always control what happens to you, you can control what you do about it. You can express yourself in those moments, maintain yourself while others react, take responsibility for your actions, create a sense of agency and autonomy within your emotional unit, and the list goes on. Executing control in those ways frees you up to respond for self. For much of her life, Emma thought she was in control because she was able to manipulate her way out of conflict. She thought everyone else was the problem. But the truth is, she really wasn't in control at all. Trying to avoid disappointing anyone, she constantly compromised her time, values, and perceived self-worth. While she was escaping conflict on the outside, she was caught in a battle within.

Emma's people-pleasing mindset stemmed from an endless desire to satisfy her parents and win their approval. Growing up, we're all told to be good boys and girls. We're punished if we do something wrong and praised if we conform with what our parents, teachers, and other authority figures expect from us. As a young girl, Emma craved her parents' approval and took pride in making them proud of her. The pleasure she got from making them proud reinforced a belief that she must act a certain way to be worthy. Since Emma yearned for her parents' love, she tried to always do the right thing. But this kept her from developing a sense of who she was and who she wanted to be apart from what others expected of her. With these experiences under her belt, Emma's sense of self vanished when she was in relationship with people.

Emma's childhood experiences formed the mindset that supported her need to put others first. She prioritized pleasing others and avoided confrontation, criticism, and ridicule by ignoring her own needs. As a result, her need to please became automatic, and she never learned how to manage the negative emotions that came with life's many disappointments. Emma learned to blame herself whenever someone else was upset; she put it all on herself to make others feel better, failing to realize that thinking this way blinded her from the truth. After therapy, Emma came to see the importance of becoming aware of herself and changing her mindset around unhelpful patterns. When you alter your mindset, you automatically change the way you feel and how you choose to react to situations. You stop taking other people's behaviors personally and start taking responsibility for your own internal experience instead.

If things aren't going well in your life as a result of your efforts to please everyone, it's time to change the way you think about who you are and what matters most in your life. It's time to start looking at the world in a different way. Dr. Wayne Dyer is famous for saying, "When you change the way you look at things, the things you look at change." Until you start seeing and thinking about things differently, you'll continue to be stuck right where you are. If you want things to change and you want to move forward in life, it's time to start writing a new story about your life—one that's based on a mindset of self-fullness rather than selflessness.

The way you think now is keeping you a prisoner of your people-pleasing ways. You've probably come up with many ways to justify and rationalize why you must comply with other people's wishes. But by always avoiding conflict, you'll never learn how to deal with anything. You won't learn how to properly manage the way you feel about disapproval. If this is something you relate to and something you want to change, you'll have to start thinking differently and responding to people in a different way. Because the truth is, you can't live your life avoiding possible conflict and discomfort without there being some serious consequences. Let me explain what I mean.

How My Mindset Limited Me

Men are not prisoners of fate, but only prisoners of their own minds.

~ Franklin D. Roosevelt

Like most young children, I grew up believing in fairytales and stories with happy endings. I believed that good would always prevail. When it came to relating to others, I didn't have a keen sense of what was good or bad, moral or immoral. I wasn't clear about the role I played in my relationships or the dreams I had for my life.

I used to think that my family and friends were testing my ability to build my own self. They seemed to be more concerned with getting what they wanted from other people than with what they could create for themselves. The goal was always to get out of doing anything difficult or unpleasant;

and I, unknowingly, played right into this. I didn't know who I was or who I wanted to be. Since my life was a constant quest to instantly gratify those around me, I bended and stretched myself to fit however I could in my relationships. The concepts I learned in my family about how to be helpful to others never really fit with what I knew, deep down, to be true. But I behaved in pleasing ways anyway. I never stopped trying to make everyone else happy, even when I realized it wasn't working. With no sense of purpose or self-confidence, I easily succumbed to being the person who always did for others.

Although I always acted with the best intentions, I came to understand that I wasn't serving anyone—least of all, me—with my people-pleasing ways. I came to understand that my hard work was actually making the situation worse. Not only was I not helping, I was actually hindering others from reaching their potential. My goal shouldn't have been to work on becoming a better problem solver. Instead, I should have been working on learning to stop doing things for others so they could start doing it for themselves. I should have been focused on being with the discomfort I felt by sitting back and not helping.

My life was spent basing my self-worth on others' opinions and relying on them to give me a sense of purpose and value. This left me feeling worthless and resentful. That's because I was taking on problems that weren't my own. I was trying to ease everyone's discomfort, including my own uneasiness around allowing people to solve their own problems. I realize now that it would have served me better to avoid giving in to my discomfort, even if it took problems longer to be resolved by others.

The need for instant approval and acceptance shows up in different ways for different people. Some people push others into taking responsibility for them, and others dedicate their lives to taking on other people's responsibilities. They either don't have the confidence to solve their own issues or don't feel good about themselves unless they're taking care of others. In both cases, they're looking outward to ease internal feelings of dissatisfaction. This was certainly true for me. I suffered many consequences for my people-pleasing ways by trying to run away from a natural part of life; but it wasn't until I decided to start seeing a therapist that I came to recognize the role I was playing in the problems causing me suffering.

Just a short time before starting my Ph.D. program, I looked my therapist in the face and felt like a fraud. I pursued a career as a therapist in order to help others. But as I spoke to my own therapist with overwhelming exhaustion in my voice, I felt upset with myself. I realized I didn't have a hold on everything in my life quite like I thought I did. I started seeing Dr. Rudes after a pretty severe panic attack.

At the time, things in my life really started falling apart. I realized this when my sense of self became blurry; I had lost myself completely and no longer knew how to keep everyone else going. I no longer knew who I was or what my goals were. If I wasn't everyone's favorite Miss Fixit, who was I? I had been working so hard in my personal life, with no positive results to show for it. I knew that my foundation was unstable; and though I always believed that if I just worked hard enough I could keep it intact, this wasn't working too well anymore. My chest walls felt like they were caving in. It was hard to breathe. It felt like a challenge to simply be alive. So there I was, sitting on Dr. Rudes's comfortable white couch, my legs barely reaching the floor, and fearing that I might actually have to show my vulnerabilities to a man I'd just met. On the outside, I remained calm and collected while answering his first question: "What brings you here today?" But on the inside, I was a nervous wreck. "Well, shoot, where do I start?" I thought.

"I had some kind of weird panic attack while driving in my car," I said. "I thought I was having a heart attack. My chest got really tight and it seemed impossible to breathe. I was seeing little white lights and had to pull over to take deep breaths. After a few minutes and lots of deep breaths, I was still alive, so I figured it wasn't a heart attack." He was curious if that had ever happened before. I told him I'd had small episodes like that when driving home from college on break. After we talked a little bit more and he told me that what I was experiencing did, in fact, sound like panic, I asked him: "So, how do I stop these panic attacks? I have a lot to do, and they're getting in the way. I've read a ton about them, and I'm open to trying anything to stop them." What he said next confused me. He asked, "What do you do to manage the chronic stress in your life?" Chronic stress, huh? Before he asked me that question, I always thought stress was stress, so I didn't know how to answer. I honestly hadn't realized I was stressed; I thought the panic attacks were an isolated problem. As soon as I got home from that appointment, I set out to research this term and started the process of figuring out whether I was chronically stressed.

When I started to research stress, I found that according to Murray Bowen, whom I mentioned earlier, there are two types of anxiety: acute anxiety and chronic anxiety. That uncomfortable feeling you get when you're driving in bad weather that alerts you to drive slowly is an example of acute anxiety. This is the form of anxiety that reminds you to act with caution in situations that might be dangerous. It's a naturally occurring alarm in your body that lets you know you're in danger, so it's actually good for your survival. When the stressor is eliminated—for example, the bad weather stops or you reach your destination— the acute anxiety stops as well. According to Bowen, "acute anxiety is fed by fear of what is; chronic anxiety is fed by fear of what might be." If you think about it, when you're anxious or afraid, it's usually because you're thinking of what *might be*. It's anticipating a bad future outcome or being fearful of the *what ifs* that fuel chronic anxiety. Chronic anxiety is an informal way to describe any type of anxiety that doesn't seem to go away on its own and isn't clearly provoked by events around you in the moment. Instead, chronic anxiety tends to be prompted by thoughts of past experiences or unpleasant future outcomes.

After conducting my research on stress and anxiety, I arrived to my next session with Dr. Rudes eager to start exploring what events might have been fueling my chronic anxiety. I shared with him one story that we both came to find pretty significant. I started, "Growing up, my grandfather spoiled my aunt. He gave her whatever she asked for. In her early twenties, she was into drugs and partying. She told me stories about how she would go to parties and they would pass around drugs. She would choose a drug without knowing what is was, and just take it like it was nothing. My aunt wasn't ashamed. She bragged to me about how everyone at the parties she'd go to would hook up with each other. 'Girls and guys, whoever was there,' she'd say proudly. Prude as I was, I always thought, wow, aren't you supposed to be ashamed of doing things like that? But she wasn't ashamed. I think those were some of the happiest times of her life."

"So, your aunt really lived a wild life," he said. "Yes," I replied. "Later in life she lived in a beautiful home in Greenwich, Connecticut. It was just her and her two children.

She was never married, therefore, my grandfather made sure everything was done for her. When she moved to Connecticut from New York City, she gained a lot of weight. It was hard for her to go up and down stairs, both because of her weight and because she smoked like a chimney. My grandfather made sure to monitor her health and was always trying to help her lose weight."

Dr. Rudes interjected, "From my understanding, your aunt was very dependent on your grandfather. Is that what I'm hearing?" "Yes," I told him. "So, dependent that a little over six months after my grandfather's death, I was woken up by a phone call at 2am. I got that 2am call while I was sleeping alone in my oversized bed. My heart was racing before I even accepted the call. 'Hello? Everything okay?' My brother answered with the words I never wanted to hear. 'Aunt Iris is dead.' I don't think my brain could even process it. Dead? That seemed so final. I mean, I had just spoken to her the other day. I looked around my dark room. I was alone with no one to comfort me, no one to talk to. I didn't even cry. I just laid there, alone in the dark."

Dr. Rudes nodded his head compassionately. I kept going. "I asked my brother, 'Are you sure?' He responded, 'They tried to revive her, but they couldn't. She overdosed on her prescription pills.' My aunt had more pills in her cabinet than a pharmacy. I always worried that she would overdose by mistake, and that day had come. But the words my brother said next took me completely off guard. 'She left a note. It wasn't an accident.' I replied, with doubt in my voice, 'She killed herself?' Apparently, her son tried to revive her, but she passed away in his arms. He found her in her room after she had taken an overdose of her prescription pills."

"That must have been really hard on you to get that

phone call. It is no surprise you're very stressed," Dr. Rudes replied. "What effect has her death had on you?" I thought about it for a moment and then said, "All of it was hard to accept. It's a good thing I still had some natural Novocain in me from my grandfather's death. Or, at least I thought it was a good thing, to just become numb. Come to think of it, I really haven't felt the impact or effect of my aunt's death yet. I didn't even realize I was so upset about everything until I started to think about why I was so stressed. It's probably because I had to take care of family business as usual, and haven't had time to think about how I feel about this loss. My aunt left me as executor of her estate, as well, and I was on a mission to sort everything out for her two kids. One of the kids has disabilities. This was a lot to deal with for me, but I felt it was the least I could do for my family."

Dr. Rudes was silent for a moment. He then looked up and said, "Because of all your new responsibilities, you haven't been able to feel the emotional effects of such a big loss in your life. It sounds like you turned off your emotions and were able to just keep going. Is this your usual response when there's a crisis?" I let this sink in and realized that it was, in fact, my usual response. When stress was high, it was always my go-to move to shove down my feelings and get to work. I thought it was because I had to be strong for others, but the truth is, I didn't want to feel the pain associated with losing someone I loved. In some ways, I benefited from keeping myself busy with others' lives, I didn't have time to be upset, feel my loss, or deal with my emotions. And the truth is, my ego was inflated by the position I held in my family as the one who held it all together. Having this position of importance gave me a false sense of calm—a false sense of self that eventually unraveled in the form of panic.

I continued to tell Dr. Rudes the story of my aunt's loss. "To the outside world, my aunt's suicide would not make any logical sense," I said. "She was a woman that was well taken care of and loved who killed herself inside her beautiful home, leaving two kids behind, with drugs prescribed to her by the so-called best doctors in her community. When she was younger, she was known as a socialite. She was simply exquisite. With long, dark, thick hair and big blue eyes, she was the envy of all her friends and every man's desire. However, I don't know if she was ever really content with her life. The only time she seemed happy was when she was on some type of drug. Believe it or not, her mind was stuck on what she didn't have. Later in life she was surrounded by people who used her; she didn't have any real friends. I think when my grandfather died, she really couldn't cope. She kept up with appearances for a few months until she reached a breaking point. My grandfather had been keeping her afloat; when he died, she drowned. She'd never learned to pick up the pieces of her life when things fell apart. She'd never developed a sense of self. So when she fell and my grandfather wasn't around, she couldn't pick herself back up." Upon verbalizing everything, I realized my aunt's story was a very sad tale. It suddenly came as no surprise that I'd been trying to suppress the emotions that came with thinking about her.

Insights from Therapy

Sometimes in life we take a stand. We take a good, hard look at our lives and decide it's time to change. Sometimes we find ourselves in circumstances that force us to figure out what we need to do next, instead of what we've always done. What I got from my conversation with Dr. Rudes is that sometimes falling down and experiencing the pain that comes with it is the only way to change. There's true wisdom in feeling, thinking about, and becoming aware of your sadness instead of hiding from the pain. There's growth in falling, in hurting, in accepting the bad. If you don't experience struggles in your life, your perspective will be limited. Your growth will be stunted. It will remain the same, even if it doesn't serve you well. Change and pain is something I tried to avoid my entire life by being a people-pleaser. If you avoid the pitfalls of life, if you hide when stress is high, you aren't creating the conditions for you to grow and mature. When my aunt died, I had to take care of family business as usual, and I didn't allow myself to feel the effects of her death. I didn't take the time to evaluate my feelings, get what I needed, and mourn the loss.

The conversations I had with my therapist led to a lot of changes in my perspective and mindset, which led to changes in my behavior. I always thought I did what others needed from me because I was a good person. The truth is, I was doing it to ease my own anxiety. Trying to escape my feelings and avoid disappointing people, I focused all my efforts on working hard to do whatever needed doing in the moment. It reduced my anxiety for some time, but in that process, I lost who I was. My true needs didn't matter. What mattered was eliminating the hurt as quickly as I could. This is the reality I'd created for myself.

My aunt seemed to have everything, but she lacked the kinds of experiences necessary for developing a sense of self-reliance. She took her life because she didn't see any way out of a recent dilemma she was in. Because everything had always been handed to her, she was never able to develop a sense of herself. Her mindset was one of receiving, because that's what all of her life experiences had been about. In some ways, I can relate to my aunt. For a long time, my sense of value and intelligence came from doing for others. I created a world in which I felt needed, and I came to believe that the people in my life couldn't survive without me swooping in like a superhero. I created that world because I needed to feel worthy as a person and because I needed to reduce my discomfort. Through therapy, I was able to understand, challenge, and change my mindset; this freed me from the patterns and perspective that were getting in the way of me living my life to the fullest.

Change didn't just happen for me. I had to work hard at it. Working hard wasn't a foreign concept to me, so I was up for the challenge; the difference was that this time, I took a hard look at my perceptions and my concept of the world. I took a look at what I was doing. I stopped blaming other people for my issues. Instead, I started to work hard on myself—not other people—and finally project self-worth, limits, and personal values out into the world. This time, my efforts started taking me in the right direction.

Through my own experience, I learned that the greatest changes begin when we look at our mindset with interest and respect, instead of judgment and denial. When we allow our thoughts and feelings into awareness, we have the opportunity to learn from them instead of unconsciously reacting to them without knowing why. We keep our thoughts relaxed by not ignoring them, and we increase our awareness of reality by being willing to encounter our personal truths. My panic attacks were a reminder that I was human. I needed to be acknowledged, and I needed to know I wasn't only valuable when I was doing for others. Our bodies have so much wisdom, and sometimes they know more than we realize.

When I first sought therapy for my panic attacks, I thought they were a sign of weakness that needed to be eliminated.

We can choose to bury our unexpressed emotions and deep thoughts, but they'll come back later, often in unpleasant ways. In my case, they came back as panic attacks. When aspects of ourselves are distanced, denied, or devalued, they'll always try to make us listen by surfacing as unwanted symptoms. Think about what some aspects of your ignored self are trying to tell you. Maybe your symptoms are coming up as chronic anxiety, depression, muscle pain, headaches, feeling lost, etc. The analogy of the missing roommate, from Bill O'Hanlon and Bob Bertolino's book *Even from a Broken Web: Brief, Respectful Solution-Orientated Therapy for Sexual Abuse and Trauma,* can help clarify the impact of ignoring our inner selves.

The Missing Roommate

Imagine that there are a bunch of people living together in a house, and they decide to kick out one of their roommate because they don't like him. They lock him out and change the locks. He comes to the door and tries persistently to get back in, but the roommates tell each other to ignore him, thinking he will go away. After a while, he becomes exhausted and slumps against the door. They think he's gone away and won't cause any more trouble. For quite a while, it seems to have worked. But he's really just sleeping outside the door. Eventually, something wakes him up, and he decides he wants to get back in the house. He pounds on the door again but gets no response and becomes tired again. Finally, he becomes desperate and crashes through the front window.

That is what happens when parts of your true self are vanished, unexpectedly. The parts of you that went missing will want to show you who you're meant to be. They'll scream, "I want to come back! I am part of you! I will not be ignored!" This is how it happened for me and many of my clients. I got so caught up in trying to be who I thought I was supposed to be, I lost who I actually was. When we devalue parts of ourselves, they develop a mind of their own. They may go away for a while, at the expense of our wellbeing and relationships, but before long they'll come crashing through the front window.

It's often the case that we have no idea what kind of reality we're creating for ourselves. We blame others for our problems, which keeps us from having to take a look at ourselves. But cutting off aspects of ourselves and attributing them to others is a form of denial. We must realize that the people in our lives are here to teach us, challenge us, and allow us to grow. How you see yourself, your life, and your options is shaped by your mindset. When I first reached out for the help of a therapist, I thought everyone around me was to blame for how sick I'd gotten. I wasn't able to see that I was the one who needed to change. I was the one who needed to grow so I could learn to better mange my life, my choices, and my emotions.

What It Means to Be Helpful

Looking back, I see that the Universe gave me just what I needed to grow and mature into a self-full person. However, I had to change my mindset and be up for the challenge. At some point in your life—and maybe that point is now—your people-pleasing behaviors will take you to a standstill. You'll have to make the decision to put yourself first. You'll need to change your mind about what it means to be helpful to others, and you'll finally stand up and start living your own life. You'll realize that you alone are responsible for your happiness and that this is true for every human being on the planet; other people's happiness isn't your responsibility.

You'll finally recognize that trying to please everybody is a losing battle that will always end in disappointment.

When I finally went to therapy, I was running on empty. But gradually, over time, I started to fuel myself with a new mindset and new ways of being in the world. I started to take care of myself for the first time ever. I started to become a self-full person. A person who can be there for others, but not at her own expense. A person who isn't invested in pleasing other people and doesn't take responsibility for how others live their lives.

Summary

On paper, my aunt had everything a person could ever need to be happy and live a fulfilled life. She was beautiful, healthy, wealthy, and loved by her family. However, the more my grandfather and other people in her life tried to make her happy, the less she experienced any happiness or fulfillment. It was mind-boggling. I often wondered, how could this be? What went wrong? That's supposed to be a happy life. Instead of ignoring my unresolved questions and thoughts, I decided to take notice of them and work toward better resolutions for my future. I inherited from my grandfather something he'd inherited from generations before him: the instinct to instantly relieve personal discomfort by reducing it for others. From these experiences, I learned to see how counterproductive this was, and how negatively it was affecting my loved ones and me. Once you realize that you don't have the power to make someone else happy—that you can only create happiness for yourself simply by changing the way you view the world— everything changes. People need to be held accountable for their own lives, and that includes being in control of their own mindset and problems.

Activity:
Developing A Self-Full Mindset

As I've already mentioned, the most important aspect of making a change is changing your mindset. Here I offer an important activity that will help you in this process. Though the questions are numbered, you can answer them in any order you like. Some of these questions will be easy to answer, and others will take some time to navigate. Take your time and answer them in whatever way suits you. Once you've responded, look at your answers with interest and respect, instead of judgment and denial. When you allow your thoughts and feelings into awareness, you have the opportunity to learn from them instead of unconsciously reacting to them without knowing why. You increase your awareness by being willing to encounter your personal truths, answering questions you never thought to ask yourself.

There are many different ways to approach these questions. Here are a few suggestions: Use a notebook and pen to journal your answers; Think about the questions, and answer them in your mind; Have a trusted friend or family member ask you the questions; Meditate with or without music in a quiet room while responding to the questions.

Ask yourself:

1

When did I first start believing I needed to please others to be a good person?

2

Who in my life would know that I am a people-pleaser?

3

How would the people in my life who believe I'm a people-pleaser describe me? Do their descriptions align *with how I feel about myself?*

4

What would I prefer to be thinking, feeling, or doing instead of pleasing others?

5

Have I ever decided not to please someone and had a good outcome?

6

When is the pull to please the strongest?

7

What would the culture within which I live have to say about the position I'm taking in wanting to change my pleasing ways?

8

How is society's view different from my own personal view?

9

What would I prefer my relationships to look like?

10

What fits for me from this chapter? What doesn't fit?

11

What difference would it make in my life if I started to apply a self-full mindset and change my pleasing ways?

Once you've answered these questions and feel you have a good grasp of their meaning and significance, I'd like you to prepare to notice the following this week: When an opportunity comes up to please, what effect does it have on you physically and emotionally? Journal about your experience, without judging yourself or trying to change anything; just take note of your process and how you feel.

_____

_____

_____

_____

_____

_____

_____

_____

_____

_____

_____

_____

_____

_____

_____

_____

_____

CHAPTER 2

. . .

Why Doing Too Much is Hurting Your Relationships

When tension mounts at work or in any relationship system, there are those who react to the tension with lowered energy levels and those, like myself, who react with increased energy. It's easy to think that the increased energy is a positive thing, but because it's driven by anxiety it gets directed in unhelpful ways which get in the way of others working well.

~ JENNY BROWN, MSW

PHIL JACKSON, THE FORMER HEAD COACH of the Chicago Bulls, understood how doing too much hinders the relationship system from functioning at its best. In his autobiography, *Sacred Hoops*, he wrote about his effort to convince superstar Michael Jordan to score fewer points in each game. Why would the head coach of a six-time NBA championship team try to get one of his best players to shoot fewer baskets? Well, he happened to have a good understanding of how relationship systems work: When someone over-functions, other members of the system tend to under-function. Over-functioning means taking on other people's responsibilities and not holding them accountable for their participation in the relationship system.

When you're doing everything yourself, you're the over-functioning person in your relationships. As a consequence of this, the people in your life under-function, doing the bare minimum and not assuming their own responsibilities. Just like a basketball team, families, workplaces, and romantic partnerships are systems: assemblies of parts that collectively cooperate for a shared purpose. However, a system is not just any group of parts: the parts of a system are connected in such a way that each is influenced by the other based on what needs to be done. The important point here is that individual parts of a system can't perform all the tasks alone, as any error or disruption will affect the entire system. Phil Jackson understood that in order for his team to win, every member had to function at a high level. If Michael Jordan, a single part of the team system, functioned at a higher level than his teammates, they would all function at a lower level.

Doing everything yourself and taking responsibility for other people in your life will—and probably already has—lead them to under-function. People need to do their own tasks and take responsibility for their own lives in order for systems to function effectively. By doing too much, you're not allowing the people in your life to function as well as they could.

The systems you participate in won't work at their best if you're trying to manage your life while simultaneously playing everyone else's part, too. Over time, you'll get overwhelmed, and other people won't have a role to play. I always thought the reverse happened: When the people in my life under-functioned, I took it as an invitation for me to over-function. I've heard countless times, especially from women about their partners, "If I don't do it, it will never get done." This is how I saw things for most of my life. If I didn't do it, nobody else would, and everything would totally fall apart. I thought this is what a responsible family member does: help others through whatever they're going through. You might be acknowledged or looked up to by others for the role you play in your relationships, but this type of approval has a major downside: it robs people of their ability to solve things for themselves.

The first step in changing your mindset and beginning to operate differently in your relationship systems is to recognize that you're only responsible for your part in your relationships. You're only in charge of your 50%. That's it. As an over-functioner in your relationships, you need to see how your behavior is unconsciously inviting others to do less. If you concentrate only on your responsibilities, resisting your natural drive to take on the stuff other people are responsible for, the under-functioners in your life are likely to respond by stepping it up. This will allow for changes in how your relationship system works. As I've said before, you're responsible only for yourself and your actions. If you want to make changes in the over/under-functioning reciprocity sequence, don't ask, how can I change my partner, friend, coworker or family member? Rather, ask, what is my involvement in this relationship system? You can continue to over-function, but it's a guarantee that nothing will change in your relationships. As Albert Einstein is credited for stating, insanity is "doing the same thing over and over again and expecting different results." I was insane for a big part of my life, working harder and harder, doing the same things over and over again, trying to get a different result. I was working so hard taking care of other people's tasks that I forgot all about my own. Over time I noticed that I only got busier and busier. The workload doesn't dwindle when you over-function; it turns out the more you do, the more you'll continue to have to do in your relationships.

If you recognize that you're the over-functioner in your relationships, here are some quick tips for you to consider:

1. Become aware of when you're doing your own tasks or taking on tasks that other people should be doing.

2. Take note of the things you're failing to do for yourself.

3. Practice sitting with the discomfort that comes with letting others deal with their own issues.

4. Hold back from trying to manage other people's responsibilities.

5. If you're used to being the person who fixes everything when anxiety is high, try to be aware of that, and hold yourself back from repeating old patterns.

The Greatest System at Work

Every time you are tempted to react in the same old way, ask if you want to be a prisoner of the past or a pioneer of the future.

~ Deepak Chopra

The human body is a perfect example of a multipart system: numerous sets of cooperating parts work together to keep us running. Each human body part has a particular task. Your eyes are there to see, your hands to bring food to your mouth, your legs to walk, etc. They are all separate parts, yet they interconnect to make you who you are. When one part of the body isn't functioning well or doing its task correctly, the other parts have to work harder to compensate for that loss.

For example, if a person becomes blind, his or her other senses become heightened. Blind people often have better hearing and are more skilled at localizing sound than people with sight. Scientific evidence shows that people missing one sense don't just learn to use the others better. The brain adapts to the loss automatically. If one sense is lost, the areas of the brain normally devoted to handling that sensory information get rewired and put to work processing other senses. Cool stuff, right? This is one example of a reciprocal interaction within a system whereby one part changes in responses to another.

The example of how a blind person's brain rewires demonstrates how parts of a system work together, stepping up and designing new ways to operate when one part can't function the way it once did. It's kind of like what happens if someone in a family gets sick; the other family members have to do more, at least at first, to work together and maintain the overall functioning of the family system. But if nobody in the family is sick, and every individual is perfectly capable of doing his or her part, things look quite different. Someone is bound to under-function if other family members are over-functioning, doing extra even when it isn't necessary. Unlike the rewiring that happens in the brain, over-functioning when it isn't necessary won't help the system work better. In fact, the opposite will happen. It's like the arms taking responsibility for perfectly capable legs and walking in a handstand all day. Not only is this inefficient, it almost guarantees that the over-functioning parts will become exhausted and worn out.

Is It My Fault People Are Under-Functioning?

It was difficult for me to realize and believe that my behavior was as much a part of the problem as was the behavior of my family members, who were always failing to take care of their own responsibilities. Just as Phil Jackson told Michael Jordan, "You've got to share the spotlight with your teammates, because if you don't, they won't grow." In the systemic view of relationships, no single person is to blame. Trying to play the blame game in relationship systems is like asking whether the chicken or the egg came first. Did others under-function and then you picked up the slack? Or did you do so much that they started to take it easy? Those are confusing questions that will take you in circles. That's why I'm offering you a new way of thinking about relationships that shows how a change in one person creates a change in another. From this alternative perspective, it's not only about why a pattern started, it's about how the pattern creates issues for the relationship system now. Looking at it this way helps all parties take responsibility for making necessary changes. Whenever there's a problem in one of your relationships, it's the outcome of a reciprocal connection between you and the person co-creating that shared connection with you. If you want to resolve the problem, it's not necessary to determine how it started or who's at fault. What matters is that both people take responsibility for their part in the process.

Being Your Own Self Within an Anxious Family

Functioning depends on how well you adapt to your environment.

~ Murray Bowen

As I've been explaining in this chapter, your family isn't just a bunch of separate people who happen to be related to each other and are just walking around in their own lives, totally unaffected by one another. Your family is, as Murray Bowen likes to call it, an emotional unit. The relationships among you and your family members are shared; each person changes in response to a processes governing those family relationships. Basically, everyone in a family is emotionally connected to one another such that what one person does affects the others. I used to believe that I was my own person, and that if I emotionally or physically distanced myself, I could prove that I was unaffected by those around me. But when I tried to put this into action, it never seemed to work. Let me give you an example that will help explain this systemic interaction and show how each person changes in response to the process governing the family relationships.

Cynthia left home to go to college in another state. She was happy to finally get away, because her family was a major stressor in her life. Throughout her life, she'd felt she needed to bear the responsibility of her family members' issues. Cynthia thought that by going away to college, she'd be free. And things did quiet down in her life—at first. However, not long after she left, her parents decided to end their marriage. This had a major effect on her, as she was pulled into the emotional battle of the divorce, despite living hundreds of miles away. She realized that the distance separating her from her family members hadn't changed a thing; she was still highly emotionally reactive to them. She realized that her need to be there for her family stayed exactly the same as it had been before she left, and creating physical distance wouldn't be enough. Cynthia decided she had to learn how to manage her own anxiety whenever there was a family crisis. Instead of trying to fix the issue, distance herself, or cut off family members, she tried to understand her family as an emotional unit and see the role she played in it. After experiencing some health issues that she felt were related to her family stress, she came to the following conclusion: "My well-being depends on understanding how I can better manage when a crisis occurs. Running away does nothing."

When people fail to develop a strong self, their well-being and functioning usually depend on what others say or don't say, instead of on what they personally want. Essentially, their sense of self vanishes in the presence of others, and they start to want to be what other people want. This all shows itself in many ways: co-dependence, self-sabotaging behavior, constant efforts to accommodate others, and even chronic inflammation in the body. After her parents' divorce, Cynthia was trying to manage the anxiety of everyone in her family by over-functioning, instead of looking inside herself to see how she was managing and feeling. She lacked a strong sense of self, so she wanted to be and do what everyone in her family expected of her. Ignoring her own needs eventually resulted in her developing an ulcer and suffering periodic anxiety attacks.

In general, people tend to be more concerned with things outside themselves, instead of looking within. I asked Cynthia, "What difference would it make if you held the belief that the people in your family could manage their own stress?" She cried out with relief, "It would be like a million bricks being lifted off my shoulders."

Change happens when you shift your experience of a problem. Whenever an issue arose, Cynthia thought she had to ease her family members' anxiety and carry all of their emotional burdens. Then, when it didn't work, she believed the only solution was to distance herself and ignore her family. In reality, she just needed to be willing to take on the challenge of looking at herself and managing only her own anxiety around the situation. Bowen emphasizes that when a difficult situation arises, what matters most is how you think about the problem, because problems are an unavoidable part of life. In Cynthia's case, she lost herself by trying to manage everyone else's stress, believing it was what she needed to do in order to help the situation. This only made her feel more anxious about her parents' divorce and more reactive to everyone around her.

In therapy, Cynthia was able to gain objectivity about the emotional process of her particular family unit. Just by thinking differently about her role as the over-functioner in the family, she was able to make significant changes. She worked with me on creating a strong sense of self—or, as Bowen would say, we helped her become differentiated.

Differentiation of Self

When we don't have a sense of self, our goal is to figure out what our environment wants us to do. By developing a sense of self, you build the ability to self-regulate and better manage your anxiety, which brings about changes that allow you to be less reactive to your family members; thus, your need for approval decreases, as do your expectations and feelings of distress. Sounds pretty good, right? It was when I learned about this aspect of the differentiation process that I decided to study Bowen's theory more in depth, which has provided great insight in my professional life, and great relief in my person life as well.

Differentiation of self is all about learning to manage your own part in your relationships with others, instead of over-functioning and trying to manage everyone else's feelings. It means being part of an emotional unit while being able to control your own functioning at the same time. Cynthia was adjusting her internal functioning to help keep her family in harmony, which had adverse effects on her health. By paying attention to her body, mind, and emotions in relation to her family, she became capable of balancing her co-occurring needs for togetherness and individuality.

Working toward becoming more highly differentiated isn't easy. You have to be motivated enough to realize your part in the family system and work on the issues yourself. The irony in all of this is that you can't differentiate a self without being in relationship. As Cynthia said, "The only way to move through it is together. Emotional distance doesn't help. Learning to manage yourself in the situation of being with the people that bring about stress is what helps. I learned to be present with my anxiety because backing away created more of it. Really, you don't get rid of anxiety; you learn how to better manage it."

When a difficult family situation arises and anxiety is high, avoiding the issue or over-functioning for your family isn't particularly helpful. This work is all about being who you want to be; that includes responding in ways that are suitable for you and beneficial to your functioning and health. It takes time and involves lots of practice with getting uncomfortable.

People-Pleasing is NOT a Positive Attribute

It's important to recognize the ways in which you're over-functioning, especially because it's not the kind of behavior we tend to think of as negative or in need of changing. The intentions behind over-functioning are good, but as I've mentioned, it hinders the effectiveness of relationships. People-pleasers are fueled by an urge to feel needed and responsible, which feeds the urge to over-function. You may be able to trick yourself into thinking you can successfully take on other people's responsibilities, but after a while, those people will rely more and more on you, weighing everybody down.

When you set appropriate boundaries and stop taking on other people's responsibilities, they're left with no choice but to complete their own tasks, resolve their own problems, and find their own resources. When people take more responsibility for themselves, it improves the functioning of everyone involved.

Thinking about your relationships this way can help you gain some objectivity about the emotional processes within those relationships, helping you make better decisions. When you first start to put it into practice, it can seem like magic, because you discover that by working on yourself and making positive changes, your relationships actually improve. Thinking in this new way will allow you to make the changes you've always wanted in your relationships, without anyone having to take any blame.

What Happens When I Stop Over-Functioning?

Once you stop over-functioning, the people in your family will either start to take more responsibility for themselves or pull someone else in to fill your former role and keep over-functioning for them. You're likely to experience some resistance, at first, from the people in your life; but after a while (depending on how persistent they are), they'll get it. In my family, most people had been under-functioning for a long time. My grandfather was the over-functioner who took care of everything in the family. That is, of course, until I took over for him. When I finally started setting boundaries with my family members, telling them they had to deal with their own issues, many of them recruited my brother to do things for them.

My brother was always very good at staying out of the way and not getting involved in family drama. He did his own thing and successfully built a life for himself. But despite this independence, his big heart makes him susceptible to engaging in people-pleasing behaviors when something is asked of him. When family members asked him for help, he figured it was the right thing to do. People-pleasers are in a constant state of vulnerability, adjusting themselves and their internal functioning to keep other people in harmony. That's why it's important to put boundaries in place and decide what's non-negotiable for you in your relationships.

Having stepped out of my over-functioner role in the family, I slowly started to see the process at work. Whenever something happened in the family, my brother would be called in to fix it. At first, he seemed okay with it; but then the nose bleeds and neck pain started, and he wasn't sure why. The reason is simple: When you do too much for other people, your self vanishes; you start to become what other people want you to be. Research shows that this kind of behavior can cause chronic inflammation in the body, along with many other physical symptoms. In flourishing relationships, people want you to be who you are, not who they want you to be. My family members wanted my brother to be the person who took care of everything for them, because that helped reduce their anxiety. They wanted him to take over my role, since I was on a journey of being self-full and no longer available the way I had once been to reduce their discomfort. As I saw this happening, I tried to explain to my brother that he was doing too much. He was initially defensive, claiming he had to do it all because I wasn't doing enough. I can see how, from his perspective at the time, he felt he needed to pick up the slack for what I was no longer doing.

My brother was frustrated, because he thought I was giving everyone more responsibility than they could handle. For example, one of the first things I did on my journey to self-fullness was have my sister start paying her own electric bill. This was a big deal and a very dramatic situation for her. She paid late a few times and almost had her electricity turned off. When my brother took over my over-functioning role, he helped her pay it a few times. He couldn't understand why I wouldn't just do it. What my brother didn't understand is that I wasn't giving anyone more responsibility. Their personal issues and bills were theirs to deal with, and it should have been that way in the first place.

The more tasks I gave my sister to do on her own, the more she asked our brother to do for her. He started to see that it wasn't just the electric bill. There was a laundry list of things she thought she couldn't do because she'd never had to do them before. Once he realized this, he started to gradually do less; eventually, she started to figure things out on her own. She now pays her electric bill and has set up her own insurance plan, completed school, and found her passions in life. It was hard for her for a while, because she had to learn things later in life and start to trust in her own abilities after years of having other people take responsibility for her. When people excessively count on others, they learn to always—whether knowingly or unknowingly—recruit people to do things for them. When they run out of options, they have no choice but to start doing for themselves. Then something amazing happens: They gain confidence in their own abilities and want to do even more for themselves.

Over-Functioning Parents

If parents over-function for their children, they undermine

the children's confidence in their capacity to take care of themselves. They unknowingly instill anxiety in their children, who don't learn that they can count on themselves and stand on their own. Parents who over-function mean well, believing they know what's best for their children. But research shows that children with so-called helicopter parents tend to be less capable of conveying what they need, solving their own problems, staying safe, and interacting closely with others. Therefore, the result of doing too much is the very thing these parents seek to avoid in the first place.

Because of my longstanding over-functioning ways, I was especially at risk of becoming a helicopter parent. I'm glad I made the transition to being more self-full before I became a mother, because I might have set my child up for a life of under-functioning. I would have continued to be confused about why I was always surrounded by people who wouldn't take care of themselves. Research shows that children of over-functioning parents fail to launch into independence because unless they're told what to do, they're uncertain about their goals, direction, and what to do next. This, in turn, raises the parents' anxiety, since they measure their self-worth according to their children's achievements. According to the research, over-functioning parents have a more negative self-perception than parents who don't base their worth on their children. These parents have good intentions, but doing too much can be harmful in the long run.

My grandfather's relationship with his two children was definitely of the over/under-functioning variety. He protected them from any difficulty they encountered or even might have encountered. He wasn't aware of the hazards of that pattern, failing to see that if he sheltered his children from all difficulties, they wouldn't learn how to solve problems on their own. As Dr. Jorge Bucay warns in *The Power of Self-Dependence*, "As a consequence, if this continued . . . by the end of the twentieth century we would have a lot of adults with a marvelous infancy and adolescence but a terribly painful adulthood."

The over-functioning / under-functioning dynamic is most apparent in the parent-child relationship. When they first come into the world, children are totally dependent on their parents. They need someone to take care of them and protect them so they can survive. But as children grow up, they start to develop a sense of self, and it's up to the parents to encourage it. Many of us are inclined to shelter our children, making things as easy as possible for them. We make it so that they don't have to struggle or manage their own lives. But this keeps them from building the coping skills they need to resolve their own issues later in life.

As a parent, my client Fred always believed he was doing the right thing for his children; until one day he came to the realization that the way he was behaving as a parent wasn't benefitting him or his family as much as he thought it was. There are few things more difficult than coming to terms with the fact that you've made some mistakes as a parent, so I felt for him when he shared this with me. As a young boy, Fred's family went through a traumatic event. He saw his loved ones suffer for many years, so when he had a family of his own, he decided that he would always take care of everyone in his family so they would never have to go through what he did. What Fred didn't understand, however, is that you can't take away other people's suffering. In fact, trying to do so may actually harm you and make things worse for the people you're attempting to shelter from the facts of life.

When Fred first came to see me, he couldn't understand

why his youngest daughter was suffering from severe anxiety and throwing tantrums when she didn't get her way. He told me, "It's like Isabella can't deal with anything. She freaks out and has a panic attack over every little thing. My family went through so much early in life and coped with it better than she copes with having to take a test at school." He couldn't understand why, after all his hard work and the comfortable lifestyle he'd created for his family, his daughter was still suffering.

It's a simple fact of life that everyone is guaranteed to experience unfortunate circumstances, some more severe than others. Most of the time, these circumstances make us anxious. There are countless things we must do on a daily basis that we don't necessarily like, and unfair things will happen to all of us, regardless of who we are. By attempting to shelter the people we love from the natural process of life, we rob them of the ability to develop the strength and resilience they need to overcome challenging circumstances. They become incapable of tolerating or managing the inconveniences of life; they demand instant gratification; and, over time, they usually develop impulse control issues. Then, when we see our loved ones suffering, we don't understand why and invest all our energy into helping them. We try harder to shelter them, instead of allowing them to be anxious and find their own way to deal with life's inevitable struggles. As writer Roald Dahl says, "The more risks you allow children to take, the better they learn to take care of themselves."

Fred was acting with the best of intentions. He thought he was being a good parent, and the last thing he meant to do was contribute to his daughter's inability to cope with difficult circumstances. While he wasn't to blame for how his daughter turned out, it would benefit both of them to see the part each of them played in the development of her severe anxiety and tantrums. Although Fred couldn't change the past, he could learn how his need to shelter and fix everything was getting in the way of his daughter's ability to manage her own life. It's natural for parents to want to protect their children from harm; it feels unnatural to watch them struggle. However, if we learn how to distinguish real danger from an opportunity for our children to explore and take risks on their own, we'll be more capable of taking a step back when necessary.

Why Let My Child Suffer?

She was the archetypal selfless mother; living only for her children, sheltering them from the consequences of their actions-and in the end doing them irreparable harm.

~ Marcia Muller

When we're caught up in the moment, it's so much easier to do what we need to do to calm our children down. However, over-protecting our children in this way can lead to worse consequences. Research shows that children who have been overly protected lack a sense of agency over their lives, are less capable of managing emotions, and are more prone to develop unfulfilling relationships. Instead of trying to rescue our children from potential harm, we can better serve them by resisting the urge to step in and take over. Modeling mature emotional regulation in difficult situations might be difficult in the short-term, but the long-term benefits are more than worth it.

The more Fred tried to ease his daughter's discomfort, the more her anxiety and tantrums intensified. Setting children up to be content in life doesn't happen by sheltering them from suffering; rather, it comes from teaching them how to self-soothe during difficult times. Fred began to show his daughter how to manage challenging emotions like anger, frustration, and, disappointment instead of trying to shield her from them. He used the skills he learned from surviving his traumatic childhood to help manage himself when he saw his daughter upset. Instead of running to her rescue, he sat with his discomfort and allowed her to get through it on her own. When parents effectively manage their emotions in front their children, they help the children develop emotional maturity.

People who can't regulate their feelings often look outside themselves for sources of soothing. They self-medicate with food, drugs, and alcohol; hold on to bad relationships; and become codependent. When they become too anxious, too sad, or too easily triggered, they end up reaching for counterproductive ways to reduce their anxiety in the moment.

Allow your children to work through difficult feelings; don't try to stop them from falling. The times we tend to get stumped with our children are usually the best opportunities for maturity and growth—not only theirs, but ours also. Children won't fall apart due to difficult emotions if you model for them what it's like to work through them. As parenting expert Robin Berman, M.D puts it, "A big part of mental health is feeling at home with your emotions, knowing that you will not have to avoid feelings, or numb them, but knowing that you have the emotional flexibility and emotional resilience to feel safe with yourself."

Summary

The health of your relationships depends on you taking care of your share and being true to yourself when making decisions. When you start moving toward only doing your part, it's important that whatever adjustments you make are in line with your values, your preferences, and your family's specific needs. You should always listen to yourself and trust your intuition when deciding how quickly or slowly you will make changes in your relationships. At first, you'll need to do what's uncomfortable and it may feel unnatural, but do it at a pace that works best for you. Remember, when we aim to please, we might have the best intentions at heart, but we often aren't being truly helpful. Contrary to popular belief, doing too much isn't good for anyone involved in a relationship system. Anyone who's capable of functioning independently should be held responsible for the part they play in their relationships—both professional and personal—and in society in general.

Just like you, I thought I was being a better person, family member, and friend by doing everything I could to make other people's lives easier. That included taking on the tasks they didn't want to do. But when I started really thinking about it, this didn't make sense anymore. If they don't want to do these things, why should I be obligated to? In the grand scheme of things, the need to please doesn't end up pleasing anyone. So you can hold on to your desire to see others happy, but realize that over-functioning behaviors won't be what makes that happen.

In the next chapter, I'll explain the importance of being yourself and show you how your authenticity will help your relationships. Please note that the intention of this book is not to change who you are. On the contrary, I want you to be *more* authentic—more of who you are. My only wish is to support you in changing how you understand people-pleasing behaviors. This way you can start utilizing your good intentions and need to please in ways that will benefit you and your relationships. I want you to see that saying yes when you want to say no is a temporary solution that leads to long-term problems. I want you to be you but also recognize that it will benefit you to change your people-pleasing ideas and behaviors.

Activity:
Changing Your Relationship Patterns

When an opportunity comes up to please or over-function, I want you to notice it and then try to do something different than your usual response. In the last chapter, I asked you to just pay attention to the feelings that come up when an urge to please arrives. This week I'd like you to notice the urge and then do something different instead of complying as usual. At this point you should be able to understand the sensations in your body when an urge to please comes up, and recognize it for what it is. Now I invite you to make a change in your response to it. For example, maybe you'll notice a pulling feeling in your gut, a headache, a sense of anxiety, or a guilt-inducing voice in your head that says, "Just do it for them."

Whatever it is you feel when the urge to please arises, identifying it will help you interrupt the pattern of automatically complying with it. If you usually do something for others without being asked, resist doing it. Instead, just sit with the uncomfortable emotions that come up, or do something on your personal to-do list instead. Organize your closet, go to the gym, or grab lunch with a friend. Do something that occupies your time instead of over-functioning for others. If someone hints at needing help with something or asks for your advice, put it back on them by saying something like, "I can see what a dilemma that is for you." If someone constantly calls and you don't feel like answering like you usually do, decline the call. The idea is to take a different approach than the one your usual over-functioning, people-pleasing nature would have you take. When the urge to please feels overwhelming and you don't know what to do, simply take a deep breath and give yourself plenty of time before responding. No action is better than your usual actions.

After about a week of engaging in the exercise I just mentioned, ask yourself the following questions: In what ways is being a people-pleaser a problem in my life? What behavior changes do I see being helpful in dealing with that problem? What is my reason for deciding to make these changes now? What are people doing in my life to pull me back into pleasing behaviors? If I were to live self-fully, what would be the first sign that a significant—though maybe small—change had occurred?

_____

_____

_____

_____

_____

_____

_____

_____

CHAPTER 3

. . .

The Importance of
Being Yourself

The Privilege of a lifetime is being who you are.

~ Joseph Campbell

"Be yourself." I used to hate when people said that to me. Don't get me wrong, it's great advice. But it isn't so helpful if you don't have a clue who *yourself* is. When you're nervous before a date, people use the advice to calm your nerves. They tell you the same thing when you're preparing for a big job interview. Heck, I know I'm guilty of saying those words to people. In fact, I'm about to do it again right here, in this chapter.

Learning to Be Yourself

We're all unique individuals. We should be able to act authentically and connect with who we are and what we value. But being yourself is only easy if you're confident in who you are. The hard part is figuring out who you are in the first place. This is especially true for people-pleasers. They often don't know what they want, because they've spent their entire lives making decisions based on other people. It's diffi-cult for them to separate what they want from what other people want. It makes sense, doesn't it?

When you're always busy pleasing others, you don't give people a chance to see who you are. To truly know yourself and be known by others, you must distinguish yourself by figuring out what your values, beliefs, and truths are, apart from other people's opinions about what they should be. You must begin to make choices for your life, instead of looking to others to make decisions for you.

How you understand yourself affects the decisions you make, and if your only sense of identity comes from the opinions or approval of other people, your decisions will be based on what pleases someone else. The words' "Be yourself" present a huge challenge for people-pleasers. Before they can be themselves, they must first figure out what they want and don't want.

Let's start with taking a look at how you know if you aren't being yourself. If you're tired of wishing you had the strength to say no, if you're overwhelmed by living a life others expect you to, if you wish you didn't have to work so hard for approval, if you don't have the courage to express your feelings or the ability to be happy with who you are, then you know you're living a life dominated by what other people expect from you. Many years can pass and lots of time can be wasted when you aren't living a self-full life. It's not so much that you'll lose yourself in your people-pleasing ways, but more that you'll never find yourself at all. If you haven't been genuinely yourself, there's a part of you that's trying to break free. This part is your intuition, the voice inside that screams at you every time you say yes when you want to say no.

Figuring Out What You Want

In this section, I offer a perspective that will allow you to see who you are, what you want, and how to make your needs a priority. Now, I'm not suggesting you only look out for yourself and forget about other people. But if you want to stop feeling stuck, overwhelmed, unsupported, lonely, and depressed, the cycle of dedicating your life to others has to stop. What I'm offering is a way to stop exhausting yourself by trying to be selfless—which only leads to resentment and exhaustion—and start becoming self-full, realizing your ability to do what you want and be who you are. This involves taking a stand for yourself, which will likely result in you feeling alive again or for the very first time. At first you must search within, which may feel selfish, in order to experience and express what you want. But over time you'll see that you can be there for the people in your life—on your terms.

In order to look within, you must first distinguish yourself from your surroundings, becoming more self-aware. Before you make any decisions—especially the decision to help someone else—you have to figure out what you want and how you want to spend your time. Self-full people make decisions for themselves automatically. But it takes time to get there. The process of defining a self, especially later in life, can be slow. As therapists and authors Bill O'Hanlon and Bob Bertolino theorize, this is because children who grow up in low-anxiety environments develop a relatively clear *sense of self*. On the contrary, children who grow up in abusive or highly anxious environments tend to have difficulty with boundaries and a tough time developing a solid sense of self. Some people don't get to develop who they are early on in life—knowing where others end and they begin—because their environment doesn't let them feel safe enough to do so. These people are left to building a self later in life, when they have the freedom, knowledge, and support to do so.

When developing a sense of self, it helps to stay in conversation with yourself, always exploring new ways to be who you want to be. You can do this by becoming the observer of your own life, which will help you be more attuned with your inner self. When a situation occurs, take a step back and watch your process, thoughts, and feelings, without trying to react immediately. For example, if someone asks you to do something or buy something for him or her, you don't have to answer right away. Instead, you can say, "Let me get back to you." This will give you some time to really consider your options, without having to make an instant decision. Your automatic response will probably be to say yes, and you may end up regretting it later.

When someone asks for something from you, saying things like, "Let me sleep on it," or "Give me time to check my schedule" lets you step away from the situation and take your time deciding what you feel comfortable doing. It allows you to observe your thoughts and feelings. Developing your ability to step away and observe a situation will promote the development of your sense of self; it will help you focus on your own emotions instead of those of other people. This will give you the option to make a choice based on who you are and who you want to be in relation to people, instead of just acting on impulse. Observing your process is part of choosing who you want to be. It separates you from the urge to please, which convinces you that you don't have a choice. But you do have a choice—in fact, you have lots of them. Do you believe you were placed on this earth to never know who you are?

I sure don't. I believe you're here to experience yourself by witnessing what you feel and value, by responding to things without self-judgment. You learn about what you want by taking charge of your part in any relationship system and acting in ways that support you when difficult situations arise.

Crisis or Growth Opportunity? Seeing Difficult Situations as Gifts Toward Self-Fullness

> *Feel it. The thing that you don't want to feel.*
> *Feel it. And be free.*

> ~ Nayyirah Waheed

I want you to reflect for a moment on the following questions: What's the first thing you do when you feel uncomfortable? What do you do, or avoid doing, when the going gets tough? And how are those behaviors working for you? Are you finding the fastest way to safety and comfort, or do you actually work through the issues that arise? Do you throw a fit? Overwork yourself? When things don't go according to plan, most of us regress, leaving ourselves behind. We allow our emotions to drive us, and we engage in automatic behaviors aimed to please others. We act on impulse to satisfy our wants, and we lose ourselves whenever something makes us uncomfortable. The real challenge for us under such circumstances is to avoid dwelling on the negative parts of life and instead think about how we can more appropriately deal with life's inevitable disappointments. How you perceive a crisis and decide to act in response to it can make the difference between effectively growing from the experience or regressing into old, not so helpful patterns.

Same Old Reactions, Same Old Results

Crisis can be averted when one can find a person
with the courage to define self, who is invested in the
welfare of the family as in self, who is neither angry
nor dogmatic, whose energy goes to changing self
rather than telling others what they should do.

~ MURRAY BOWEN

My client, Jenifer—a self-proclaimed people-pleaser, over-functioner, and perfectionist—knew exactly what she did when her anxiety was high and she felt things weren't moving the way she wanted them to. She went into fixing and lecturing mode, overstepping her boundaries and inserting herself into other people's lives. When a difficult situation arose, her automatic reaction was to find ways to resolve the issue immediately, even if it wasn't her issue to solve. This made sense to me, because people-pleasers tend to lose themselves in the process of automatically jumping into action to help others—especially when they assume something bad will happen if they don't. Pleasers try to eliminate the possibility of a negative outcome by immediately disconnecting from their anxious feelings and running to the rescue. They don't want to feel uncomfortable, and they don't want others to hurt, so they go into fixing mode. But as Jenifer soon found out, this doesn't work so well. That's because, paradoxically, the more you try to run away from something unpleasant, the more you stay connected to it. Also, the reality is that nothing truly gets resolved when you insert yourself into other people's battles as a way to relieve your own anxiety. When you do this, you aren't acting for self. You aren't acting for others' benefit, and you aren't growing either. You're just doing the same old thing in order to minimize the bad feelings you're experiencing in the moment.

Helpful Tips to Remain Self-Full During Crisis

When a negative situation arises, instead of disconnecting from it immediately by going into thoughtless action, look within yourself and ask, "What type of person do I want to be in this situation?" Think about how your best self would like to respond, instead of how your impulse for comfort would prefer that you act. Then do what you think or believe is right. Or, alternatively, do nothing. Like I've said before, sometimes it's okay not to respond. However, always take a moment to acknowledge and appreciate the situation instead of giving in to the urge to do something about it.

When you're faced with difficult situations in life, try to see them as opportunities for you to decide who you are and see what you're capable of. As Neale Donald Walsch says in his book *Conversations with God: An Uncommon Dialogue,* "Each circumstance is a gift, and in each experience is hidden treasure." When you continue to act in certain ways just to gain approval and avoid hurt, you rob yourself of the opportunity to experience who you can be in different situations and circumstances. How you choose to behave, think, and feel are all expressions of who you want to be. When you observe your *self* without judgment or impulsivity, you're making a decision about who you are; you're being self-full. Situations in life, even negative ones, can always serve as opportunities. When you can start to see them that way, you'll no longer need to engage in harmful behaviors to avoid them. Instead, you'll be able to be more mindful and thoughtful in your responses. You'll be an active participant in your own life instead of a leaf blowing in the wind.

There are a few ways that you can practice acting self-fully when a crisis arises, allowing yourself to move through setbacks without creating more drama in other aspects of your life:

1. Make a real effort to have your feelings line up with your logical brain by looking at the facts of the situation.

2. Practice sitting with the discomfort that comes from your wants not being immediately satisfied.

3. Think about your personal values instead of imposing them on other people.

4. When people in your family system upset you or you don't agree with them, try to stay connected to them rather than pulling away.

5. Remember that you are not responsible for other people's problems, and they need to find their own way.

6. Have your own ideas, values, and thoughts even if others disagree with them.

7. Look beyond your initial impulsive reactions so you can see your real intentions, and act in ways that better fit with who you want to be versus what your impulses dictate.

Respect Your Inner Self; Allow People to Do for You

During the process of creating your self, you must remember that you can't go through life trying to please everyone around you. You also can't go through life terrified about what others are going to think. I mean you *can* go through life that way, it's your choice; but you already know where that road leads. Whether it's your style, opinion, beliefs, or possessions that others judge, you can't allow their judgments to stop you from trying to experience who you are. If you let this happen, you'll no longer be you. You'll be living a lie, being whoever everyone else wants you to be. Everybody deserves to have relationships that involve a balance of giving and receiving—even you. It can be awkward, at first, to allow others to do for you, but that's a big part of what love is. It's part of what a healthy relationship is, too.

It took me many years to understand that concept, because for much of my life I didn't feel good enough, and I compensated by doing too much for other people. Perhaps you can relate. You think you don't deserve the same amount of love and acceptance that you offer to others, so you do more to prove yourself. This helps you keep from feeling rejected and alone. The people in your life may be very critical of you, so you try to be perfect to appease them. This doesn't allow you to take your needs into account. This doesn't allow you to be a part of your relationships.

People-pleasers judge themselves unrealistically. They believe they have to be perfect in order to have value. It may be that we do this because we carry around the critical voices of our parents, grandparents, friends, teachers, or other people we've looked up to. We want those voices to stop, so we do more and more to prove ourselves. For example, my client Maria, lived most her life by the book, exhausting herself with efforts to be perfect, just to avoid upsetting anyone. She explained that she always felt like a show horse, being watched 24 hours a day; Maria had to be constantly groomed, maintain her posture at all times, and always have everything perfectly aligned. However, she wasn't living by her own rules, but rather by the strict family rules that had been clearly written out for her. This left her no room for errors, regrets, or confrontation. As a result, there was no room for growth, accomplishment, or excitement either.

As Albert Einstein said, "Everybody is a genius. But if you judge a fish by its ability to climb a tree, it will live its whole life believing that it is stupid." That applied to Maria. She felt stuck in a cycle of pleasing that she couldn't see a way out of, because she didn't want people to see she wasn't perfect. When you know and respect your own inner self, you're clear and confident about who you are, flaws included. You also know the actions that do and don't fit with who you want to be. Maria tried to set boundaries, but her efforts to please everyone kept her from maintaining them. She felt incapable of asserting her limits with the people in her life. After therapy, she came to understand that she's only human; of course, she isn't perfect! "I know that it's okay to have flaws—and actually, I prefer it that way," she told me.

Know your limitations, be understanding with yourself, allow others to know you. You'll probably always have an innate urge to please, but the urge will feel less and less powerful over time. Once you start accepting who you are, you'll realize that the voices of your critics disappear, and the truth about who you are is the only thing that matters. Other people's criticisms will bother you less and less over time, and that urge to please won't be so bothersome, because you wont have anything to prove. You know who you are, flaws included. Give yourself time to evaluate how you want to respond to situations that might provoke your urge to help, and figure out who you want to be in relation to others.

Individuality and Togetherness

Being self-full includes balancing our need for individuality and our need for togetherness in our relationships. When we're acting selflessly, our togetherness urge pushes us toward others for attachment and approval. When the togetherness is too intense, we may pull away from people too much or lose ourselves in the relationship. This is an automatic process for people-pleasers, especially when we are highly anxious. However, as human beings, we thrive on connection so it's important to not totally disconnect either. Striking this balance comes with knowing who you are and what your values are apart from others. Once that's clear, you can be in relationship with others while maintaining a sense of who you are as an individual. From this awareness, you can be the person you want to be in your relationships. In other words, the core of who you are won't have to change according to who you're with at any given time.

Do you change based on who you're in a relationship with? Do you change your needs or interests so that people will like you? I once worked with a client who would change the type of clothes, food, or music she liked based on the guy she was dating. She had no core identity and would create a new self to fit with whoever she was with at the time. She would give herself up so completely in her romantic relationships that she had no idea who she was when she was alone. Her relationships never worked, because they were based on an anxious need to complete herself with her partner, constantly seeking his approval. What took her time to understand is that she could never get from another person what she should be giving to herself. No one else can truly tell you who you are, what you value, what you like or dislike. You—like everyone else—deserve to have your own identity, even when you're in a relationship. Nobody benefits when you compromise who you are.

When you first start trying to become more self-full, you'll push toward defining yourself as separate from others. You'll move toward adopting your own beliefs, values, and choices.

You'll have a real sense of autonomy. For selfless people, building a sense of self that includes personal beliefs, goals, and boundaries is a difficult process. You need to become aware of your boundaries, especially the ones that are non-negotiable in your personal relationships. When you discover how to be yourself, you'll stop looking for someone else to complete you, because nothing else will be lacking from within.

The more self-full you become, the easier it will be for you to manage your natural, opposing impulses for autonomy and togetherness. You'll feel complete, even when you aren't in a relationship. You'll become comfortable with who you are, without having to give in to what other people want. Tom was the type of person who always had to be in a relationship; he went from boyfriend to boyfriend. Other people thought it was just because he was irresistible and that men just couldn't wait to be in a monogamous relationship with him. However, Tom knew the truth. He felt worthless unless he had a boyfriend. After some sessions with me, during which I explained Murray Bowen's theory of *differentiation of self*, he found that he compulsively sought relationships in an attempt to complete himself the same way he'd seen it done in his family. This was dangerous, he explained, as he was seeking relationships as a way to complete his incomplete self.

Entering an intimate relationship in order to gain approval or validation is risky, because it can mean failing to set proper boundaries. It might mean allowing yourself to be treated in ways that are unacceptable to you. Tom felt stuck in his relationships, because he knew that the men he was with could have done any number of hurtful things to him, and he'd stay with them out of fear. He often felt stuck in his relationships, but he couldn't end them because he worried it would make him feel even more lost. It's important to have parts of yourself that are solid, unchangeable, and non-negotiable in your relationships so that you never feel imprisoned by them.

Once you become self-full, you'll no longer feel the *need* to be in a relationship, and you won't let go of parts of yourself to be with another person. This is different from compromising, which doesn't involve giving up parts of who you are. When you act selflessly, you give up who you are to please others so they won't disapprove of you. If you are in a relationship as an attempt to complete yourself, your wellbeing will depend completely on the approval of your partner. And that's no way to live.

Remember, Your True Self is Perfect

Michelangelo said, "Every block of stone has a statue inside it and it is the task of the sculptor to discover it . . . in every block of marble I see a statue as plain as though it stood before me, shaped and perfect in attitude and action. I have only to hew away the rough walls that imprison the lovely apparition to reveal it to the other eyes as mine to see it." That's how we should view ourselves. Just as the artist can see the art inside the block of stone, you should see the potential inside of yourself. So often, all we see of ourselves is a block of unfinished person. We sometimes don't know how to chisel away the heavy rock that's hiding our beauty.

With all the pressure we get from society and the people around us, it's easy to get caught up in ideas about how we're supposed to be. We get so many messages about how to dress, what kind of music to listen to, and how to respond to life in general that it's hard to hear our own voices in the mix. Growing up in Miami, Melanie was constantly sent the message that you aren't of value if you don't have a nice car, house, or designer clothes. When you're young, it's easy to feel that you aren't good enough unless you own the latest and greatest electronics, have a particular body type, or look a certain way. Melanie could feel herself wanting things without really knowing why. Part of her knew that it wasn't in her nature to need to wear expensive jewelry, drive a luxury car, or carry a designer handbag; but somehow she found herself feeling that she wasn't worthy unless she had those things. Melanie was willing to compromise herself in order to feel the sense of worthiness and belonging she believed would come from having all the right material things. That's how strong the desire to fit in and belong is—especially when you don't know how special you are, just the way you are.

Figuring out who you want to be, in the midst of external messages telling you who you should be, is an ever-evolving process. But that process starts with **you**. Now is the time to invest in yourself and make your desires a priority. It's okay to take time and think about what this all means, to truly observe your own life and start listening to your inner voice. When I first started defining my self, I decided to start managing my life instead of managing other people's lives like I'd always done. I learned the magical power of declining phone calls and responding to texts with "I'll get back to you." What I found is that if you just give it a little time, other people will find a way to resolve their own issues. While you let that time pass, you'll get the space you need to gain a better understanding of what you want in order to start living a life that's congruent with who you are. There's nothing better than working toward your best self and your best life every single day. The Buddha put it best when he said, "A man who conquers himself is greater than one who conquers a thousand men in battle."

Learn to Love Yourself

I want to start this section with a beautiful poem by Charlie Chaplin on self-love. It flawlessly expresses what I'd like to express to you about how important it is to love yourself and how wonderful the results will be once you do it.

AS I BEGAN TO LOVE MYSELF

As I began to love myself I found that anguish and emotional suffering are only warning signs that I was living against my own truth.
Today, I know, this is "AUTHENTICITY".

As I began to love myself I understood how much it can offend somebody
As I try to force my desires on this person, even though I knew the time was not right and the person was not ready for it, and even though this person was me.
Today I call it "RESPECT".

As I began to love myself I stopped craving for a different life, and I could see that everything that surrounded me was inviting me to grow.
Today I call it "MATURITY".

As I began to love myself I understood that at any circumstance, I am in the right place at the right time, and everything happen sat the exactly right moment. So I could be calm.
Today I call it "SELF-CONFIDENCE".
As I began to love myself I quit stealing my own time, and I stopped designing huge projects for the future.
Today, I only do what brings me joy and happiness,

*things I love to do and that make my heart cheer, and I do
them in my own way and in my own rhythm.
Today I call it "SIMPLICITY".*

*As I began to love myself I freed myself of anything that
is no good for my health—food, people, things, situations,
and everything that drew me down and away from myself.
At first I called this attitude a healthy egoism.
Today I know it is "LOVE OF ONESELF".*

*As I began to love myself I quit trying to always be right,
and ever since I was wrong less of the time.
Today I discovered that is "MODESTY".*

*As I began to love myself I refused to go on living in the
past and worry about the future. Now, I only live for the
moment, where EVERYTHING is happening.
Today I live each day, day by day, and I call it
"FULFILLMENT".*

*As I began to love myself I recognized that my mind can
disturb me and it can make me sick. But As I connected it
to my heart, my mind became a valuable ally.
Today I call this connection
"WISDOM OF THE HEART".*

*We no longer need to fear arguments, confrontations or
any kind of problems with ourselves or others. Even stars
collide, and out of their crashing new worlds are born.
Today I know THAT IS "LIFE"!*

In order to even consider the process of becoming self-full, you need to love yourself. And you begin loving yourself when you start to create who you are in every situation you face. When you start prioritizing yourself, instead of thoughtlessly catering to the needs of others, you have the opportunity to love yourself. That alone can bring about incredible transformation. When I read Charlie Chaplin's poem, I was inspired. I felt a connection between the sentiment it conveys and the ideas I want to share with you. The poem invites us to ask ourselves, Do I really love who I am and who I'm becoming? I want you to hold that question in your mind when making decisions on a daily basis. Pay attention to the circumstances that are brought to you, and become more mindful of your responses. Ask yourself, how have my people-pleasing behaviors kept me from living a happy life? Do I think I don't deserve the love that I so openly give to others? Do I believe I have to do what people say, or else they won't love me—or worse, I won't love myself?

Loving yourself comes about when you learn to accept what happens in your life as part of the process of growth that leads you to your potential. When you love yourself, you face life head on and don't hide behind people-pleasing behaviors. You're able to overcome all of life's setbacks, because you have faith in your ability to get through them.

Is It Too Late for Me?

You're never too old, never too bad, never too late, never too sick, to start from scratch once again.

~ BIKRAM CHOUDHURY

A woman in her 70s came to see me after her husband passed away. Her three kids were grown and out of the house with their own families. She was lost and confused about what to do next. What was her worth if she wasn't caring for her kids or doing what her husband wanted? To this woman, having so much freedom of choice didn't seem like freedom at all. It felt like an actual death sentence. She would say, "What do I do now? I have no idea who I am or what I want. It's too late for me anyways."

The current population has a longer life expectancy than ever before. Many people, from many different generations, are aging. And as they do, they're repeatedly questioning who they are and who they want to be. My grandfather was clear minded and strong until he was 94 years old. He sometimes struggled with the newer generations and once said, "Now I know why we don't live forever. The world changes too much. This isn't the same place I was born into." He didn't give himself enough credit. He was using email, trading stocks, exercising, and playing cards with his friends every week. He was living in this new reality and slowly changing over time; without realizing it, he was part of this new world too, and he continually found new ways to enjoy himself.

Sometimes we take a stand and decide it's time to take a good look at our lives and change. Sometimes we find ourselves in circumstances that force us to figure out what the heck we need to do next. My client was perfectly fine with her reality of living for her husband and children. Her lifestyle fit the expectations for women in her generation and was consistent with the ideas she grew up with in her family. She took care of the kids, her house, and her husband; her husband took care of the bills and made most of the major decisions. But sitting in my office after his passing, she asked herself a question that she'd never asked before in her 70 years of living: "What is it that I want?" That can seem like the scariest question in the world. We think it should be freeing to be able to answer that question. We think the answer is just floating out there someplace, waiting to be grabbed. We think it should be easy to answer questions like, What do I want? Who am I? What is my passion? We fight many battles to be able to answer these questions for ourselves. To be free with so many options can be suffocating and feel like a lot of pressure to people who've never believed they have the option to ask themselves those questions or examine their lives. Once you decide it's time to find out what you want, it's time to start.

Thoughts can either keep you stuck or open up opportunities for you that you never thought were possible. If you think it's too late for you or that it's just too much work, you'll be trapped, unable to move forward. You can force yourself to change your thoughts and use them to lead you into uncharted territory, no matter how old you are. Freedom of thought allows you the opportunity to follow your unrealized passions. But first, you have to get rid of the idea that freedom isn't an option for you. You have to know that it's possible for you to make your needs a priority.

Summary Checklist for Becoming Self-Full

- ✔ Change to a self-full mindset
- ✔ Connect with your self
- ✔ Realize that self-fullness isn't selfishness
- ✔ Change negative ideas about yourself
- ✔ Change your definition of being helpful
- ✔ Stop over-functioning
- ✔ Remember the importance of being yourself
- ✔ Figure out what you want
- ✔ Respect your inner self
- ✔ Remember, your true self is perfect
- ✔ Love yourself
- ✔ Remember, it's never too late

Activity:
Being Yourself

This week you'll be practicing being an observer of your own life. When opportunities arise to please, instead of immediately reacting, you'll simply observe the situation. When observing from the outside, you can look at the situation from a more objective standpoint, instead of an emotional one. Looking at situations logically allows you to make better decisions. When observing a situation, seeing it for what it is, ask yourself this question: What would my best self like to do in response? Then do that.

At this point, it's helpful to be aware of the following: the sequence of how your pleasing behaviors take place, and what other people do and say that triggers you to please. It's also really important to realize that the world doesn't fall apart if you don't run to the rescue. If you're not aware of the effects of your pleasing behaviors, I'd like you to go back to the previous chapters and work on the other activities for a while, until you have a better understanding of the process. There's no time limit on any of these activities; they're intended to help you gather information to support you in this process.

Once you're clear about the process, you can ask yourself the following questions when an opportunity to people-please arises: What would my best self like to do right now? What actions would make me happier? What type of person do I want to be in this situation? What does my inner self want to do? You don't have to answer all of these questions. Choose the ones that fit for you, according to your particular circumstances. When something arises in my life that requires my attention, I always ask myself, who do I want to be in this situation?

Take obstacles, situations and interactions with people as an opportunity to express who you are, who you want to become, and how you want to express your true self. The only way to really know who you are is to try on certain actions for size and see how they make you feel. Over time, you may notice that acting in ways that fit with who you are simply feels better than acting in ways that don't naturally align with your true nature. This exercise will allow you to continue making better decisions for you and your future.

_____

_____

_____

_____

_____

_____

_____

_____

_____

_____

_____

_____

CHAPTER 4

. . .

Letting Go So You Can Be Free to Be Self-Full

To let go does not mean to get rid of.
To let go means to let be. When we let be with
compassion, things come and go on their own.

~ JACK KORNFIELD

HOLDING ON TO PAIN doesn't fix anything. Replaying the past over and over again doesn't change it, and wishing things were different doesn't make it so. In some cases, especially when it comes to the past, all you can do is accept whatever it is you're holding on to and then let it go. That's how everything changes. You have to let go of what's hurting you, even if it feels almost impossible to do. Deciding to hold on to the past will hold you back from creating a strong sense of self—a self that isn't defined by your past, but rather by who you want to be.

Oddly enough, painful feelings can be comfortable, especially if they're all you know. Some people have trouble letting go of their pain or other unpleasant emotions about their past, because they think those feelings are part of their identity. In some ways, they may not know who they are without their pain. This makes it merely impossible for them to let go.

Before my client Martha came to see me, she'd been holding on to negative emotions related to her past for so long that most of her current relationships had been negatively impacted. She'd allowed her life to be defined by her bad childhood, and even though she was in her 40s, her mind was still back where it was when she was eight years old, living in her childhood home with her abusive father. Time continued to pass, but her childhood wounds remained open. How is that possible?

We've been told that time heals all wounds. But time is just time. If you don't allow yourself to heal and move forward, many years will pass but your pain will stay the same. The distance between the years doesn't make healing happen; you heal by changing your relationship to the past. When Martha spoke about her childhood, she was still very emotional about it, as if she were still living it. Although life had moved on, she'd stayed behind, locked in the past thinking only of the bad times. What she and others don't realize is that whether or not you choose to let go and take a chance on living a life without anger or pain, time passes. Life goes on.

Some people feel like victims for so much of their lives that they have a hard time letting go of that idea of themselves. They muddle through life full of pain, anger, and resentment, never wanting to forgive the past. Because of this, they don't live in the now. When I think about the ability to let go of being violated, hurt, or wounded, I think about the survivors of the Holocaust. I know from personal experiences with survivors that we can learn a lot from their stories. The people who truly lived were those who found a way to move forward with their lives, refusing to allow the Holocaust to define them. When I listen to the stories of Holocaust survivors, I often hear a similar message: "We must forgive but never forget." It took me a while to understand that idea, but what I gather from it is that in order to move forward, we have to forgive the people who have wronged us. Yet we can't forget what they did, because we must protect ourselves from letting it happen again. The act of forgiveness isn't for the person or people who have wronged you; it's for you, because you can't have peace without it. You can't grow without it either.

Martha was able to find peace in her life when she decided to look back, accept, and forgive what had happened to her. When she realized that her father's actions stemmed from unresolved issues from his past—and his unwillingness to forgive the abuse he had suffered as a child—she realized the abuse would only continue if she didn't resolve it herself. Martha suffered intense emotional pain throughout her youth, so she couldn't understand why she kept recreating the abuse she suffered in her adult relationships. Without healing her past, she wasn't able to find satisfying relationships or live a fulfilling life. Sometimes you have to look back, with a changed perspective, to move forward and let go. This helps assure that you don't continue the mistakes from generations before and instead resolve the past for a better present and future. It's almost guaranteed that your relationships will mirror the pain of your past until you resolve what needs to be resolved. This is a path that every person experiences in unique ways, and everyone must sort it out for themselves.

There Is No Self-Fullness Without Forgiveness

My grandfather was born in 1914 in Nidda, Germany. He grew up on a farm with his mother, father, and younger sister. He was a smart child who worked hard in school and always dreamed of going to college. His mother pushed him to study, and he even learned how to speak English. At 17 years old, he was ready to attend college and had good enough grades to get into any college he wanted. But because he was Jewish, he couldn't go to any of them. Before the war, his mother decided to send him to America on a boat to start a new life where being Jewish wouldn't be an obstacle.

He lost 16 family members in the Holocaust and was able to save his sister and parents from perishing as well. He could have adopted the view of his oppressors, that Jews were nothing but trash to be thrown away, but instead he relied on himself and made a new life for himself and his surviving family. He never let the ideas of the Nazis define who he was. He wasn't going to be told he couldn't make something of his life.

When he got older, he told me he was still alive because he was Jewish. I thought that was a strange thing to say. Most of his family and friends died because they were Jewish, and here he was believing he was alive because of it. He told me that if he hadn't been Jewish, he would have stayed in Germany and fought in the war. Everyone he knew in Nidda who wasn't Jewish died in the war. If he wasn't Jewish, he would have never fled or made a life for himself in America. He was able to live 94 years because he was Jewish; that's the story that defined him.

With my grandfather's way of thinking, I could forgive just about anyone—even the girls who bullied me in middle school. His perception of what happened allowed him to define the events differently, and because of those perceptions, time actually did heal his wounds. By the time I was born and got to know him, he wasn't angry or resentful. In fact, he went back to Nidda and made friends with the mayor and priest of the town. My grandfather went back not for revenge or hate, but to build a monument and museum for all the lives lost in the Holocaust. He didn't do this with anger; he did it with love and forgiveness in his heart. He did this because he was able to let go of what happened, so he could experience who he was and wanted to be. He developed a memorial to remember the many lives lost so that people won't forget what happened and will ensure it doesn't happen again. He overcame that horrible event, because he didn't allow anger or hatred to consume him. He allowed his true self to show in the face of adversity.

I once had to learn to let go. For years, I wished evil upon the girls who brutally picked on me in middle school. I would repeat to myself, "What goes around comes around," as they would throw pencils at my neck in class or whisper, "You're stupid" in the hallway. My heart was filled with hate for them, and I wanted them to suffer like I had. I would write in my diary about the emotional pain I was feeling as I cried every day after school. The only thing that would get me through it was thinking it would end and comforting myself with the belief that one day they would feel the pain I was feeling. Have you ever felt so angry that you wished harm on another? Anger is what happens when you don't want to be vulnerable to your pain. Anger is a strong emotion used to keep us from feeling hurt. When people respond to situations with anger, there's more to the story. Behind their anger is a fear of being hurt, a fear of not being able to stand up for themselves, or a fear of unjust or unfair things happening. These are all reasonable feelings. However, when those rational feelings are masked by anger, there is no space for forgiveness—or for you. Only when the anger subsides can there be room for forgiveness, letting go, and having the ability to act based on your values and beliefs.

Goodbye Anger, Hello Me

With Forgiveness, your victim identity dissolves,
and your true power emerges.

~ Eckhart Tolle

One night at a friend's party, I went into the bathroom to find one of my bullies on the floor crying. To my shock, I asked her, "Are you okay?" She told me the other girls had turned on her, and I realized she might be suffering the same fate I had. She looked so sad, and all I could think was, "Wow, the moment I've been waiting for is here." She was crying just as I had cried so many nights. But I was surprised to find that seeing this didn't make me feel nearly as great as I thought it would. In fact, it didn't feel good at all to see this girl suffer the same way I had. I sat with her so she wouldn't be alone. She apologized for everything she had done and promised she would never make fun of me again. For a few weeks after that, I let her sit at the lunch table with my friends and me. It provided a big lesson in that awkward stage in my life: Holding on to revenge, anger, and hatred may get you through the tough days, but at some point you must let it go so you can live your own life apart from the pain. You can't properly heal when you're still angry. Anger is a sign that the wound is still wide open. Like the saying goes, "Healing doesn't mean the damage never existed. It means the damage no longer controls our lives, and the wound has turned into a scar." Even though my bully eventually went back to her old ways, I healed from my anger and desire for revenge. This made room for me to be able to create a clearer sense of who I wanted to be apart from it.

Getting through my emotional suffering allowed me to find forgiveness and make it through about three years of bullying. Instead of writing in my diary about my sadness, I started to write about how my life would be once the bullying was over. I started to appreciate that even though I wasn't considered cool, I had friends, and they were great to me. I accepted where I was in my life and let go of the past. I put all my energy into being a better student and a good person so that I could help others one day. We do not have to be victims or slaves to our pain forever. We don't have to let others' harmful actions control or define who we are. We can change our narrative and see the negative events differently, allowing them to shape us in ways we never could have imagined when we were in pain.

As Buddhist teacher Ajahn Chah explains, when we choose not to follow the path of letting go, we choose to carry a heavy rock around with us, weighing ourselves down. We don't know what to do with the rock, so we just keep carrying it around. When someone insists we throw it away, we think, "Ahh if I throw it away, I won't have anything left." We hold on to our negative feelings and pain, carrying them around with us and refusing to throw them away. Even when others explain to us the benefit of throwing away the emotions— or the rock, as Chah puts it—we're still afraid to let it go. We've been carrying it for so long that it's become a part of us. So we continue to carry it around until we get so weak and tired that we have no choice but to let it go. Only when we've had the experience of letting something go can we fully understand what letting go means. It's only then that we can finally feel at peace and recognize how physically and mentally heavy that rock really was. You'll never be truly happy if you continue holding on to things that make you sad. You'll never be able to experience a self-full life if you're weighed down by anger. Don't allow the past to control your present and future. As Mooji, a spiritual teacher originally from Jamaica, said, "Feelings are just visitors, let them come and go."

People-Pleasers Accept Others' Ideas of Themselves

If you're stuck in the past and can't let go of things that happened to you, chances are you're accepting what your abusers, bullies, or other negative people in your life believe about you. If you don't start letting go of their ideas about you, you'll be imprisoned by them, never able to live to your full potential. For many years, I was stuck acting in ways I thought would make me fit in or gain people's approval. It took me a long time to realize that other people's thoughts and ideas about me had more to do with them—their beliefs, issues, and opinions—than with me. Other people's viewpoints are manifestations of their unresolved issues and anxieties; they have no bearing on the facts of who you are. Putting others' opinions above your own ideas about yourself devalues your worth and makes their word stronger than yours. Your ideas, and the way you experience yourself, should take center stage. In my experience, I've found that people with dominant parental figures have a harder time valuing their own ideas over others' ideas about them.

My client Carl's father is loud and forceful about his views, and his mother is extremely opinionated. Though they never directly forced Carl to be a certain way or think a certain way about himself, they were always loud and critical when he did something to displease them, leading him to believe that he needed to act in certain ways to make them happy. When we're young, we want to please our parents. That's all Carl ever wanted to do. He lived according to his family's rules and tried desperately to please his parents. But he learned that pleasing them was a losing battle; nothing he could ever do would be good enough for them. I'm sure that if you have similar parents, you've also learned there's nothing you can do. It's exhausting to continue trying to mold yourself into someone other people will be satisfied with—especially because some people will never be satisfied, no matter what you do.

Try as you might, it's impossible to completely please another person. This is particularly true when the person is dealing with his or her own demons. Critical people wear selective lenses that only let them view the negative aspects of what you do. They fail to recognize that something positive can be found in almost every situation, person, and event. Maybe in the short run you can do a few things right in their eyes; but over time, you'll realize that it's impossible to get it right in their eyes all the time. And in reality, their inability to be pleased has nothing to do with you or your worth as a person. This is something Carl had to learn the hard way. After many years of trying to please his parents, his heart broke at accepting that he could never make them happy.

In college, one of my psychology professors showed the class a picture of a child's bedroom. He asked us what we saw in the photo. Some students said, "A pile of dirty clothes" and others said, "A beautiful photo on the wall." Some noticed other things, good and bad. The professor then went on to say that he could tell who was generally optimistic and who was generally pessimistic based on how they described what they saw in the photo. It was the same picture of the same room, but everyone had a different perspective of it. Most of the students saw what was wrong with the picture, not what was right with it. This isn't surprising, because most people are trained to see what's wrong with life, people, and events. So if you base your value on how others view you, you'll find that you don't end up valuing yourself very much. Carl lived many years without valuing himself. He had a lot of great qualities and accomplishments to make him feel proud, but as long as he was waiting to get his parents' approval, he would never approve of himself. He would never be able to see all that he had done.

Just like Carl eventually learned to do, it's helpful to let go of the idea that you must be a certain way so that others will accept you. And you most certainly have to let go of the notion that their acceptance will make you good enough. As soon as Carl stopped apologizing for being himself and became confident in himself and his decisions, other people's opinions started to impact him less and less. He was able to make decisions based on what he wanted. Carl now considers himself to be in recovery for people-pleasing, overachieving, and perfectionism. He remembers that every time he makes a major decision, just like an alcoholic has to remember he or she is in recovery before going to a party where alcohol will be served. He now makes sure that his decisions are based on what he wants and not what pleases others.

Carl explained, "People say to me all the time, 'You don't seem to have bad effects from your childhood.' Well, let me tell you. It most certainly did affect me. It's just that I didn't act out in the traditional rebellious way. Instead, I internalized my pain and worked myself to exhaustion trying to be good enough for my parents, my friends, my teachers, and society as a whole, when I should have just been trying to be good enough for me." Like Carl pointed out, when you start to be good enough for yourself, you can let go of the need to be accepted by other people.

The Cost of Living a Self-Full Life

Part of being self-full is understanding the part you play in your relationships, then separating more of a self from others, without emotionally distancing yourself. Once I started living for myself, I got a lot of pushback from the people I used to do too much for. When that happened, it was hard for me to not emotionally distance myself from my family when they were angry or upset. They were used to me being in a certain role, so the changes I made presented a challenge for them. I don't think they liked me very much for a while. They struggled when I started to live more for myself, because they were used to me always putting their needs before my own. My changing meant that they had to make changes too. I shook up the family and now joke that it was the price I had to pay for my freedom. Before I was living for self, I would stop everything to listen to my family members when they were upset. I'd do tasks they didn't want to do, and run to the rescue if they made a mistake—which, unfortunately, seemed like a daily occurrence. When I started saying, "I'll get back to you," or, "What are you planning to do about it?" instead of doing it for them, it didn't go over too well with the people who had grown accustomed to relying on me. And honestly, I get it. That's the role I'd always played in my family system. I co-created their dependence on me through my habitual responses to them. Now who was I to just stop doing what I'd always done?

The moment you start living your own life, for yourself, will be a definitive one for your future. But don't be surprised if you start feeling like people are waiting in line to tear you down because of it. I know that sounds dramatic; but, unfortunately, it feels that way. While people may not consciously or intentionally try to harm you, they'll try everything to get you back in a position where you'll be available to please them. Since your people-pleasing nature had many people relying heavily on you, their anxiety will rise when you don't comply—and when people are anxious and believe you're the cause of it, they usually get angry with you. When you people-please, you place your life in other people's hands. You work only for their approval of you. But sadly, they won't take the time to try to understand you and appreciate the good parts of you, because they'll be too concerned with what you can do for them. Chances are the people who need the most pleasing from you are not very concerned with your feelings at all. They're only accustomed to getting their wants met immediately. They need the pleasing you're giving because they never learned how to offer it to themselves. And guess what? If they aren't offering it to themselves, they won't be offering it to you either.

When people get upset with you, the trick to maintaining your composure and not reacting angrily is to remember that this is all part of the process. The ability to avoid lashing out or reverting to old behaviors is gained through a long process of training your intellect to take over for your own natural reactions. When emotions are high, just try to observe the predictable process at work. If you know it's coming and remind yourself that it isn't personal—because people's reactions are all based on their individual issues and anxiety—you'll be better prepared to respond in a more relaxed manner.

As I've been saying, once you stop trying to please others and start doing things for yourself, you'll feel a strong pull from people who resist and resent your changes because they're not being served by them. That's what happened to Shirley when she first started building boundaries. She found herself having to deal with confrontation and criticism for living her own life. When that happens, you can easily revert back to your old patterns. But if you do, you won't be able to experience life as yourself. Anything worth having in this life comes at a price. It isn't easy to change; that's why so many people don't do it. Mostly, it's hard to change when people you care about don't seem to support you at first.

Wanting to keep the peace in her family kept Shirley trapped for a while. It may be keeping you trapped, too. I gave Shirley an example, from her favorite movie, to help her understand why keeping the peace was actually hurting her in the long run. I said, "What would have happened if Mel Gibson's character in the movie *Braveheart* would have tried to keep the peace? What if he didn't try to fight for his freedom?" When she heard that, it clicked. She grew up thinking it was wrong to disagree with people. "Having my own opinion was never a valuable option for me. I thought of violence as horribly immoral," said Shirley. "Think about it," I said, "what if your freedom, values, worth, and right to make your own decisions were threatened? Should Mel Gibson's character have just watched while his country's women were being raped, their land stolen, and their freedoms taken?" Shirley replied, "No!"

When you're dealing with demanding people, it's often, unfortunately, their way or the highway. I'm not saying they're bad people or that you need to go to war with them. But it's helpful to look clearly at your relationships and see if always giving in, like Shirley did, is helping you live your own life or hurting you. Building a strong sense of self is essential to that process, which also involves getting comfortable with the idea that disagreement can be constructive. The idea that confrontation may actually be beneficial to you and your relationships probably seems totally outlandish. I get it. That's exactly what Shirley and most of my clients thought, too.

In order to overcome your fear of confrontation, you must change your perception of it. Happy relationships aren't those in which conflict is avoided; they're the ones in which conflict is dealt with productively whenever it arises. Conflict is unavoidable in intimate relationships, but there's a difference between constructive and destructive conflict. Speaking up is having the ability to express your authentic feelings, in a logical way, which is an important part of maintaining closeness and intimacy. People who fear confrontation tend to feel alone, helpless, and unheard. That's because they don't allow themselves to tell people what bothers them. As psychotherapist Harriet B. Braiker, Ph.D. puts it, "Happy couples handle conflict constructively to advance the goals and needs of the relationship." People-pleasers just avoid it at all costs, which doesn't allow their relationships to reach a deeper level.

Once Shirley decided to start to speak up in her relationships, she began to see a significant change in her life. She now understands that this as a continuous process, which starts with learning how to engage in constructive conflict instead of always aiming to keep the peace. As she explained it to me, "One of the most valuable lessons I've learned in therapy is that if handled correctly, disagreement can be healing and beneficial."

When we don't manage ourselves through conflict, we either internalize our feelings, which negatively affects our bodies, minds, and energy levels, or we release our anxiety by reacting in negative ways. Avoiding conflict keeps us from properly handling whatever is bothering us; it starts to eat away at us and usually creates more issues over time. For me, suppressing my feelings meant suffering from anxiety attacks, muscle inflammation, migraines, and chronic fatigue. It takes a lot out of a person to suppress unpleasant feelings instead of managing the discomfort and expressing it rationally. At first, suppressing emotions might seem like the easier way, but it's worth changing that response over time—for the benefit of your health and your relationships.

Fear of anger, disappointment, or confrontation tends to result in debilitating consequences—all because of an attempt to keep a false sense of harmony in your relationships. Saying yes when you want to say no, and seeking approval from others are actually harmful to your health and your relationships—the same relationships you were originally working hard to protect. That's because you, as a people-pleaser, are adjusting yourself and your internal functioning to keep everything copasetic. But here's the good news: There's a way to get along with family members and keep your relationships close, and you don't have to stuff down your feelings or get into screaming matches to make it happen.

When you learn how to have conflict constructively, you benefit from feeling better, because you finally experience being able to self-regulate and thoughtfully consider the most helpful response to the situation at hand. This helps advance mutual understanding in your relationships, and may lead to fewer problems in the future. When expressing yourself constructively, it's helpful if you concentrate on expressing what you think about the situation instead of blaming or attacking the other person. This minimizes the escalation of anger and creates a safer environment for you to discuss your differing opinions. It's important to remember that constructive conflict is a way to learn from your experiences in order to reduce the occurrence of similar issues in the future. It isn't a new means of placing blame on yourself or the other person.

Destructive conflict is an upsetting and draining experience; so if you've been attempting to ignore it, that's perfectly logical. Some people in your life may get very defensive when you bring up your concerns, making you fearful about sharing them. This will make it extremely difficult for you to effectively address your issues and fix what needs fixing. Below are some tips for learning how to overcome this fear and share your concerns, even with defensive people.

4 Things to Remember When Overcoming Your Fear of Confrontation

Don't Bury Your Feelings: Start seeing your inclination to avoid confrontation as the main indication of relationship trouble. Don't be scared to disagree constructively. Rather than shouting, the thoughtful way to express yourself is to reflect on the question, How are we impacting each other? Look within to see what part you played in the situation and what actions you can take to engage in a constructive conversation about it.

Remember That Conflict is Inevitable: Don't judge yourself or think something's wrong with your relationship if a conflict occurs. A certain amount of conflict is typical in any relationship. It's impossible to keep all your relationships conflict-free. Instead of trying to avoid conflict, you can learn how to face situations constructively, without allowing things to escalate. Until they're addressed, the same issues will keep arising.

Don't Be Afraid: Your experiences have taught you to be afraid of anger, conflict, and confrontation. But you don't need to be fearful. Instead, find effective and helpful ways to communicate how you feel when anger and conflict arise.

Stop Overestimating Other People's Anger: Your fear of confrontation causes you to overestimate how angry others will get when you express yourself to them. Some people may very well get upset; but usually, your imagination is exaggerating how angry they'll become. Your only responsibility is to bring up, in a rational, clear manner, what you think about a situation. How the other person responds is out of your control.

If you aren't able to make clear what you want and express how you feel in your relationships, those relationships—and you—will fail to mature. Your relationships will lose their authenticity, honesty, and intimacy, which are all necessary ingredients for healthy human connection. If you're caught up in worrying about other people's feelings, you won't be able to express your own feelings and let people know when you're angry, hurt, or feel violated. You'll begin to resent other people, which will keep your relationships from flourishing. You might even cut certain people out of your life when they let you down, which is isolating and counterproductive. Our pleasing impulses must be challenged so we can contain our emotional reactions and bring them under the supervision of our logical brains. Remember, conflict isn't a bad thing that must be avoided. If it's done correctly and handled with maturity, it allows you to make meaningful connections, let go of whatever's been bothering you, and deepen the intimacy of your relationships.

Learning to Let Go

So, how exactly do you start the process of letting go? Once you understand that what people do and say isn't personal—rather, it's most likely a reaction to unresolved stuff from their own past—you can take it less to heart when they act in ways that upset you. Just because we're nice to people and act in respectful ways doesn't entitle us to be treated the same way. I know, I know. That isn't great news. But the reality is, your kindness doesn't immunize you from other people's projected unpleasantness. Instead of investing yourself in avoiding negative reactions from other people, start directing your energy toward learning to let things go. You do this by being present to what's going on inside of you, rather than obsessing over how someone is going to react to you. If your mind is invested in the outcome, you'll miss out on the process of deciding how to act for self. Similarly, if you're caught up in worrying about how other people will respond to you, you'll fall into the trap of manipulating your response in order to please them.

I became the master of saying exactly the right thing at the right time to please other people and get them to like me. What resulted from this was that people liked the fake version of me, and I lost touch with my true self. I also ended up avoiding a lot of conflict, which as you already know, doesn't serve anyone. It's hard to be yourself and express yourself when you're always worrying about how other people will react to you.

You have to have trust in the process, let things be, and believe that things will work out. Situations usually unfold the way they're supposed to, and worrying about worst-case scenarios never helps. Trust in the greater plan for your life, and believe that things unfold over time as they should. I used to have a habit of reading the last pages of a book before starting to read the actual book. I always had to know what happened at the end before I could relax and just read. But I've come to learn that in life, we have to move past the urge to jump to the end of the story and just enjoy the present moment. What choice do we really have anyway?

Life is more exciting once you learn to let go of trying to control everything. If you don't learn to let go and instead continue changing yourself for others to avoid getting hurt, all you'll really be doing is trying, unsuccessfully, to control the situations and people around you. It's actually quite manipulative to change your reaction to people based on the response you want to get from them. It undercuts your functioning and theirs, as well. A big part of letting go is getting comfortable with the unknown and realizing that you really don't have control over other people anyway. As the saying goes, "If you actually want real control, lose the illusion of control."

Letting Go When Someone Hurts You

It's especially hard to let go when someone has—or continues to—hurt you. However, it's important to keep in mind what I said earlier: When someone does something to hurt you, it's more about them than it is about you. And the truth is, even though it sucks, it's okay to hurt sometimes and reflect on that hurt instead of rushing to do something about it. If you continue to act for yourself, learning to distinguish between your emotional reactivity of the situation and your thoughtful response to it, you won't be as sensitive to criticism. It's harder to live in fear of people's reactions than to actually live your life, despite that fear, and try to sort out your feelings to others' reactions afterward. I had a client whose mother treated her siblings completely differently than she treated her. When I asked her why she thought that was, she said, "My mother knows that if she ever said to my siblings the things she said to me, they would never speak to her again." Her mother would take all of her frustration and anger out on her, knowing that her people-pleasing nature would compel her to just take it. Of course, that didn't make it right for her mother to treat her that way, but it certainly contributed to the dynamics of their relationship. Now, in adulthood, my client recognizes that she only has control over how she chooses to respond to her mother and how she allows herself to be treated. Her people-pleasing didn't ward off her mom's criticisms; it only intensified it. My client would never be treated with respect if she continued to answer to her mother's demands without telling her how she was affected by them. One day, my client finally told her mother, "Enough already!" Over time, after many conversations, her mother learned a more appropriate way to treat her.

What you tell yourself about a situation will ultimately determine whether you forgive and move on or stay angry. If you honestly don't believe that people do things to be evil and think they're mostly just unaware of how their actions impact others, it will significantly influence how you respond to them. People will never know what you're thinking if you never tell them. If you look beyond blame and see each person as part of a system of mutually influencing relationships, you'll have a better time understanding the role you play in the hurt you've been feeling. People took things out on me because they thought I could handle it. It was natural for them to make that assumption, because I never spoke up or said anything. When you don't say anything or set boundaries, you become a non-entity who gets used as a doormat. Just as you deserve respect, the people in your life deserve the respect of knowing that what they're doing hurts you. Letting them know puts it out in the open. If they do it again, you must be consistent in setting the proper boundaries. Some people will get it right away, others will take longer, and some may never understand. Be clear about what you need from the people in your life, over and over again, until they understand. Distinguish yourself, and be responsible for your 50%. Remain close, open, and vulnerable.

People-pleasers have a tendency to tolerate other people being rude to them, keeping quiet about it until one day they explode. When that happens, the other person is usually surprised. Nobody will know what bothers you if you don't tell them. That's why communication is so important. It's hard to forgive, let go, and move on until you sort out and become aware of your emotions about the situation. We live in a culture that supports getting all your emotions out right away. That's not what I'm talking about either. I'm suggesting being aware of your emotions, sorting them out on your own, waiting for your immediate reaction to settle down, and then expressing your thoughts. When you decide to do that, you can't be invested in the outcome or overly concerned about how the other person will react to you. At that point, it's out of your control.

I make it a point now to speak up to the people I care about and let them know how their words and actions impact me. I used to be scared, because I didn't think they would understand; I assumed they would just get mad at me. However, over time, I noticed that setting boundaries in a firm, rational way made it so that they respected me more and started being more considerate of my feelings. I noticed that the less I focused on other people's reactions, the better their reactions would be. It's important to think about each situation in a logical manner, rather than being led by your emotions. Nothing ever gets accomplished when emotion-based decisions are made. So make sure to confront the people you love when you're able to think rationally about your contribution to the situation, and not when you're feeling fed up and angry. Use your judgment to guide you in deciding when the timing is right to confront the people you love.

Tips for Letting Go and Becoming Self-Full

Understand that the relationships you thought you'd have are going to be different than the ones you actually have. Accept the person you are in this moment, and start accepting other people, too. As time goes on, you'll continue to learn that things don't always go as planned—actually, they pretty much never do. And that's okay! If you become aware of the part you play in your relationships, those relationships will improve. Practice gratitude and appreciation. Trust in the process of life. Whenever things haven't turned out the way I planned but according to the universe's plan instead, it's always worked out for the best.

Don't be invested in the outcome when it comes to dealing with people, because it often leads to disappointment. Expectations have a way of keeping us stuck, because they lead us to fear certain outcomes. There are no guarantees in life, and there's nothing we can really do to get the outcomes we desire when dealing with others. When our expectations or needs aren't met, we need to respond rationally and appropriately. Sometimes this means setting respectful boundaries; other times it means letting go.

Don't live in chains when you have the key. We live with self-limiting beliefs that we let define who we are. We think, "I could never do that! I could never make that happen!" If you truly believe that, you'll never accomplish your goals. Open up your mind and allow yourself to believe in yourself. There will be many people who tell you that you can't do it. It's up to you to prove them wrong.

Let go of the idea that you can control others' actions. We really only have control of ourselves and how we act. You can't change another person, so don't waste your time and energy trying to. I think this is the biggest factor that pushes people to please. We think, "If only I do everything for everyone, they'll never get mad at me." Wrong!

Only worry about what you think of yourself. Free yourself from being controlled by what other people think. Start to prioritize how you feel about yourself. As Mahatma Gandhi said, "Happiness is when what you think, what you say, and what you do are in harmony." You can't live by your values if you're living for the approval of others.

Leave room for mistakes. Did you make a mistake or say something stupid? It's okay! I used to avoid saying something stupid and was always on edge to say the right thing. Now I cut myself some slack and laugh about it. Use the experience to learn and make a joke. It doesn't make you stupid to say something wrong or silly; it makes you human, and sometimes even funny.

Accept the things you cannot change. Stop wishing things could be the way they once were. Bring yourself into the present moment. This is where life happens. You can't change the past; you can only make decisions today to help how your future turns out.

Don't take yourself too seriously. This will allow you to relax and enjoy life's journey. I laugh with myself and at myself all the time.

Do what scares you. Fear holds us back from doing a lot of things; it closes our minds to possibilities for the future and locks us into our comfort zone. Most fears fill us with doubts and what ifs that imprison us. The more you do to get out of your comfort zone, the more your fear will subside. Do what scares you, and you'll be surprised by how much you grow and succeed!

Express what works for you. Find your voice and share with others what you're thinking and feeling in a rational way. If you continue to communicate with others what works for you and doesn't work for you, you'll no longer bottle up your emotions. Expressing yourself is an important part of feeling good about yourself and your relationships.

Allow yourself to feel negative emotions. Whether you lost a loved one through death or a break-up, honor your loss. Trying to ignore your negative emotions will extend your suffering. Loss is difficult to experience, and it's okay to allow yourself to hurt and be sad. Let yourself feel and go through the grief process so that you can move forward.

Learn forgiveness. Resentment and unwillingness to forgive will keep you locked in the past and prevent you from moving forward with your life. Remember: When you forgive, you aren't doing it for the other person; you're doing it for yourself. If for no other reason than that, forgive and let go.

Summary

You may be having trouble letting go of your pain, past, and negative emotions. Without realizing it, you might think these things are integral to your identity. In some ways, you might not know who you are without your pain. And, of course, it's nearly impossible to let go of something that you think is part of who you are. Famous Swiss psychiatrist and psychotherapist Carl Jung said, "I am not what happened to me, I am what I choose to become." There's a lesson in that for all of us. Try to let go of whatever it is that's holding you back from experiencing your Self. You'll probably realize that you are not what other people say you are. You are not your pain, your past, or your emotions. It's usually negative ideas about ourselves and hurtful self-talk that get in the way of who we really want to be. Being able to let go requires a strong sense of self, which gives you the ability to better govern your need for approval from others.

Creating a strong sense of self allows you to not put so much value on what other people think of you. Because people will think and say negative things about you when you don't act in ways they expect from you. Knowing yourself and loving who you are will help you better manage your emotions when things get tough. Here are a few crucial aspects of *not* accepting what others think of you:

1. Becoming comfortable with who you are; 2. Not putting so much value on others' opinions; 3. Realizing that other people don't know more than you do, and you can be right, too; 4. Recognizing that other people's opinions say more about them than they do about you; 5. Learning that it's okay to say and do things other people don't like, as long are you're being true to yourself; and 6. Letting things go. Those ideas will carry you through your journey to self-full living. In the next chapter, I'll talk about not ignoring discomfort and actually experiencing your problems so you can grow.

Activity: Letting Go

In this activity, you'll be working on letting go, which will afford you the ability to confront others about how you feel in a more constructive way. Think about a situation from the past that you've had a hard time accepting—something someone did to you that still hurts when you think about it. What effect did it have on you? What did it make you believe about yourself? What difference would it have made in your life if that situation never occurred? I want you to bring up those feelings from the past that you've been having trouble releasing. What are they telling you? It may be helpful to journal about these feelings or speak with a trusted friend, family member, or therapist about them.

Now consider what that experience has taught you about yourself. Do you like what it brings out in you, or do you hate how it makes you feel about yourself? Consider writing a letter to your past self. Explain all the emotions that the situation brought about for you. Describe how you wish things would have played out, and write about the person you are today because of that situation. Write about what it would look like if you found forgiveness. Confront yourself in your letter; let yourself know how that situation made you feel and what you wish you could have done differently. When you think the letter is complete, read it out loud to yourself, then fold it and place it in an envelope. When you're ready to let that part of your life go, rip the envelope into tiny pieces. Find a ceremonial way to release the letter and say to yourself, "I am letting this go now. Goodbye." When the situation tries to invade your mind again in the future, say to yourself, "I've let you go. We've said our goodbyes." Then concentrate your thoughts on the ripped and scattered pieces of paper, and let it go.

CHAPTER 5

· · ·

Avoiding Problems Doesn't Allow You to Grow

The foundation of all mental illness is the unwillingness to experience legitimate suffering.

~ CARL JUNG

WE TEND TO THINK the main point of life is to just get through whatever problems we're facing so we can be done suffering once and for all. We can't wait to arrive at our happily ever after, where sadness is a thing of the past. However, most of the time, our problems don't really get solved. We muddle through and just cope with life the way we always have. Most of us find a way to manage life's challenges without engaging in much deep thought; we simply keep doing what we normally do, even if it isn't working. Instead of solving our challenges, we maintain them; we don't make them worse, but we don't make them any better either. Life comes together for some time, then falls right back apart again. Then things come back together again, only to fall apart once more. If you think about your life thus far, I'm sure it has played out that way. As Pema Chödrön explains in her book, *When Things Fall Apart: Heart Advice for Difficult Times,*

"Personal discovery and growth come from allowing room for all of this to happen: room for grief, for relief, for misery, for joy, for happiness, and for love." When you make room for all situations to occur—good and bad—you can start to think about the most effective way to deal with the challenges you face. You can consider how you would like to respond, and how you can maintain your sanity while you face those challenges head-on. You can practice learning to manage yourself in uncomfortable situations instead of distancing yourself from them. You can lean in to anxiety, knowing that backing away just creates more of it in the future. As Henry Ford put it, "Most people spend more time and energy going around problems than in trying to solve them."

Suffering comes from wishing things were different and believing that happiness should be a 24-hour state of mind. It comes from not accepting the facts of life and failing to look at our own behaviors. From this perspective, most of our misery is self-inflicted. We expect the ideal to overcome the actual, and we expect things or people to be different so we can be happy. One of the tricks to contentment and self-full living is letting the tough stuff happen and allowing life to be difficult sometimes—trusting in the process, and self-managing through the storms. As Pema Chödrön teaches us, "It is important to allow the bad things to truly affect you. Let experiences change you, the hard moments inform you, and the pain to be your teacher." The experiences in your life are trying to show you who you are. Please, don't ignore your discomfort. Don't run away from yourself. Don't focus on what brings you instant gratification. Instead, lean in to the difficult experiences; allow them to be part of your life.

As Murray Bowen famously said, "We all have an infant inside of us, but the infant doesn't have to run the show."

Many of our immaturities, which come into play with our need to get our way in the moment, show themselves within our relationships. Our fear of vulnerability leads us to gravitate toward experiences and people that comfort us and make us look good. We emotionally distance ourselves from people who are more difficult to deal with, even if they're important to us. When we make a choice to avoid people or situations that might make us uncomfortable, we limit our growth potential. We stay close to people who don't challenge us and avoid situations that seem problematic—the very situations that offer us opportunities to truly grow into ourselves. This is not self-full living.

Numbing Yourself to Life

When my grandfather passed away, I became numb and started going through life like a robot. I went through the motions without much feeling. Some people turn to drugs when they don't want to feel anything. I got the numbness without taking any substances to induce it. At the time, it seemed like a good thing to escape pain. But when you don't feel the bad parts of life, you can't feel the good ones either. That's just the way emotions work; the switch is either on or off. If you turn off your emotions, you turn away from the possibility of sadness, but you turn off happiness, too. If you're on autopilot doing things for other people all the time, chances are you're not really feeling life; you're avoiding it altogether. That's not living.

When I started to make decisions for myself and do what works for my life, I started to feel alive again. When I accepted that life is going to be hard at times, and most things are out of my control, I could hear the music on the radio again. I could truly feel the pain and joy of life. I was able to grieve the loss of my grandfather and feel the bliss of welcoming my first child into the world. When my grandfather was buried, I thought my chances of having a good life were buried with him. But unlike him, I was given a second chance at life, and I finally realized that the opportunity to take advantage of it was only in my hands.

As I said before, your way of thinking about life and what it means to be helpful needs to change in order for you to feel free. We live in a world that privileges instant gratification and the masking of pain through substances. It's all about feeling good now and doing what fills our urges in this moment. It's the basis of addiction, which stems from a legitimate urge to avoid feeling pain and escape whatever's bothering us. My addiction was feeling needed by other people and escaping through their problems. I was also avoiding the pain associated with disapproval, criticism, and not being liked. My sister's addiction was drugs. She would avoid feeling any ounce of pain by smoking marijuana; as she got older, this hindered her development and ability to cope with life's normal difficulties. I would tell her she needed to change and stop using, but I was actually doing the same thing—just in a different, more socially acceptable way.

When life gives you a bad situation, instead of jumping to find relief, honor the struggle and appreciate that it's a crappy predicament. Nothing gets better by wishing things were different and wanting your life to be perfect. Looking back, I realize that my need to please derived from my desire for everything to be perfect and to avoid seeing others suffer. I thought if I could just solve all the problems, everything would be okay. But that's not how it works. Taking others' suffering away from them doesn't solve anything. It just increases your anxiety and makes other people more dependent on you, ultimately raising their anxiety as well. People need to learn how to rely on themselves, and you need to learn that it's okay to allow them to do it.

We must become aware of the dangers of avoidance behaviors and change our relationship with pain, problems, and anything uncomfortable. It only makes our problems worse when we revert to our childish impulse to find the fastest way to ease our discomfort. Forget about society's ideas about masking pain with prescription drugs. Start experiencing life, with all the good and bad it brings. We only make things worse for ourselves when we avoid problems and try to get rid of them immediately. It keeps us from realizing what they're telling us. It keeps us from learning how to manage in future difficult times. And it keeps us from being true to ourselves. When my grandfather died, it was totally normal for me to be upset, lost, and vulnerable. At 24 years old, it was okay for me to be overwhelmed and not have all the answers about investments, trusts, and estates. It was alright for me to not know how to deal with estate planning that came with a lot of emotional baggage. I thought I had to show courage and strength, but what I didn't realize at the time is that sometimes courage and strength means throwing your hands up and saying, "I'm lost. I need help." It's not becoming emotionless and pressuring yourself to have all the answers, trying to solve the problems of the world instead of the one that's right in front of you. I didn't want to hear the voices of disappointment or see the people I care about struggle. I didn't want to believe that I wasn't perfect. Real strength comes from listening to your pain, finding ways to manage during those times, and watching your own anxiety without suppressing, avoiding, or passing it on to someone else. It's important to remember that when you make changes to improve your life, you're going to feel some anxiety. Be patient! Your journey toward agency, autonomy, competency, and maturity isn't an easy one—but it's definitely one worth taking.

Letting It Be

Founded in 1958 by Don D. Jackson and some of his colleagues, the Mental Research Institute (MRI) is one of the founding institutions of brief and family therapy. It's also among the leading sources of ideas in the fields of interactional/systemic studies, psychotherapy, and family therapy. According to MRI researchers, problems come up and stay because of the way we mishandle them. A central tenet of the MRI approach to therapy is that people's attempted solutions to their problems may actually be the problem. Have you noticed that when we try to fix things, everything just seems to become even more of a mess? By trying to categorize and tidy things up, we muddle everything even more than if we'd just let it be.

In his book *Steps to an Ecology of Mind*, Gregory Bateson writes, "Now I suggest that the last hundred years have demonstrated empirically that if an organism or aggregate of organisms sets to work with a focus on its own survival and thinks that that is the way to select its adaptive moves, its 'progress' ends up with a destroyed environment. If the organism ends up destroying its environment, it has in fact destroyed itself." Our attempted solutions to survive may actually be the very thing destroying us. Instead of living with our environment, we try to control it, and by trying to control it, we're ultimately destroying it. By being a people-pleaser, you're trying to control your relationships. You're attempting to solve problems that aren't yours to solve in the first place. By doing this, you're hindering your ability to be happy and limiting the happiness of the people in your life, too. When you see people having a hard time and rush to take over for them, you're attempting a solution that will only make things worse.

We must learn how to stop doing things for other people that they're fully capable of learning to do for themselves. We must question what true support means and consider what is truly helpful. We must become aware that our efforts to support our family, friends, co-workers, and spouses may actually be maintaining the problem. We must realize that truly doing good sometimes means sitting back and allowing other people to step up. When we learn to tell the difference between helpful and unhelpful support, we gain the strength we need to let people resolve their own problems.

There are two important things to keep in mind in order to keep your urge to resolve everyone's problems at bay: (1) problems get maintained over time through unsuccessful efforts to get rid of them, and (2) how you orient to problems that arise changes your ability to deal with them. Have you ever noticed that the harder you try to fall asleep, the more awake you feel? Or the more you attempt to suppress an unwanted thought, the more intense the thought becomes? Have you ever tried to cheer up a depressed person, only to find that the person becomes sadder? The attempted solution adds to the problem so that eventually, the problems and attempted solutions become intertwined in a vicious cycle. To resolve the problem, you need to apply less of the same solution.

My sister's attempted solution for the problems she was facing was using drugs to cope and feel better. However, the more drugs she used, the more problems she would have, which would lead her to use even more drugs. This happens for people-pleasers, too. The more you attempt to solve others' issues, the less capable they'll be of solving issues for themselves. This plays into the cycle of exasperating their problems by creating more difficulty for the people that haven't learned to deal with their own issues. This will require you to step in even more to solve things for them. The more attempts you make, the harder it will be for you to break the cycle. When I talk about problems, I'm not talking about the small things you can fix right away, like putting air in your tires or paying a bill. I'm talking about the issues in your life that keep returning to haunt you—the ones you keep unsuccessfully attempting to resolve.

When my grandfather and aunt passed away, my solution was to become emotionless and go into people-pleasing mode. Whenever difficult situations came up, I numbed myself by running to someone's aid. That attempted solution wasn't working for me, but I kept applying it anyway. Down the road, things only got worse. I gave up on knowing myself and hindered the growth of my family in the process. At the time, I wasn't even aware I was doing it. It took my body blasting me with pain for me to finally try to figure out what was going on with me and my relationships. Now whenever I'm upset and want to jump into action, I sit back, play some relaxing music, do some writing, or go to the gym. I stay where it's uncomfortable, make no attempts at fixing it, and regulate my emotions. It can feel impossible to just turn off your usual automatic behaviors, so instead of turning them off, replace them with something different.

Being a people-pleaser is your attempt to avoid something in your life that hurts you or could potentially hurt you in the future. For example, I was trying to ignore that I was mourning significant losses in my life, that I wasn't perfect, that I didn't have it all together, and that I didn't know my worth unless I was doing for others. To become more self-full, you have to take a moment and see what's going on with you so that you can deal with it instead of ignoring it. Each circumstance is a pathway to self-fullness, and it's up to you to figure out how to navigate it all. Take note of the attempted solutions that aren't working for you, and do what you can to change them.

Developing a Systems Perspective

Gaining more knowledge of one's distant families of origin can help one become aware that there are no angles and devils in a family: they were human beings, each with their own strengths and weaknesses, each reacting predictably to the emotional issue of the moment, and each doing the best they could with their own life course.

~ Murray Bowen

As I've been saying, you don't fix problems through mindless actions; you fix them by changing your perspective and responding to situations in more helpful ways when they arise. The problem isn't only the actions you take, it's the thoughts, feelings, and sense of urgency behind those actions. By changing how you perceive your role in your relationships, you'll create a shift in those relationships. Bowen's concept of differentiation of self, which I've mentioned throughout this book, will give you a basic systemic understanding of personal growth that will shift your perspective. Essentially, people who are differentiated have the capacity to think autonomously while remaining connected to others. Within a systemic understanding of human behavior, the only way to define yourself is within the context of your most important relationships. Systems theory explains the fluctuating ability everyone has to stabilize their emotions and logical brain, balancing their desire to be connected with their desire to be independent.

As you may have noticed, Bowen's theory isn't an easy one to grasp. Throughout this book I've offered approachable explanations of his ideas to support your journey into self-full living. Bowen's ideas allowed me to see the world through the perspective of each of my family member's, instead of being limited to my own subjective experience. This helped me start taking other people's actions and mistakes less personally. Seeing the bigger systemic picture moves us beyond finger-pointing and helps us see the relationship forces that set people on their unique life paths. This way of understanding our lives and relationships provides a necessary means of defining ourselves through our relationships.

Bowen's concept of differentiation has been shown in research to enhance personal wellbeing, relationship satisfaction, stress management, decision-making, and the ability to cope with life in general. In his research, Bowen found that families manage stress in patterned ways that are remarkably similar to the instinctive ways other species handle threats to their packs. Bowen theorized that our problems derive from an instinctive reaction to things that might threaten our relationships. If we gain objectivity about our instinctive processes at work, we can learn to change our responses and make meaningful changes in our lives. When we gain a clearer sense of self, we become less reactive and less in need of attention and approval from others. We gain the ability to self-regulate within the emotional system of our families. When we're willing to be honest about how we relate to people, our lives and relationships benefit tremendously. Looking at the relationship patterns within our family systems is a great place to start; it reveals the problems that get repeated from generation to generation.

If you've ever tried to understand the issues you're currently facing in your life, you might have gone down the road of thinking about how they were influenced by your early life experiences. This might have led you to blame your current hardships on your parents. When you think in simple, cause-and-effect terms, it's easy to blame your parents for just about everything. I mean, they were the ones who raised you, after all, and they might have done some pretty irresponsible things. If you've ever had thoughts like, "I'm needy for love because my parents never showed me affection," "I don't know how to pay my bills because my parents were always bad at managing their money," or "I have a fear of commitment because my parents' marriage didn't work out," you're certainly not alone.

It makes sense to consider how our parents contributed to the issues we face as adults. However, before we place all the blame on them, it's important to consider the position they held in their own families of origin. In other words, it's important to ask, How did their parents shape their paths and lead them to become the people they are? What challenges did they and the generations before them face? Your parents were kids once too, and throughout their lives they've faced issues similar to the ones you face in your life. When you think about your parents in this way, it might invite you to look at the bigger picture, seeing them as humans.

I'm going to say something that might be difficult to understand, but I hope you'll follow me: Most of your parents' reactions to you have come from unconscious efforts to relieve their own anxiety, not from evil attempts to screw up your childhood and adulthood. Your parents inherited patterns of relating to their loved ones, just as you did. You might be thinking, "Okay, but even if that's true, it doesn't make it any better. Will understanding this make the things they did to hurt me go away?" Honestly, probably not. I say that with compassion, because I know it's got to be hard to read if you had a particularly difficult upbringing and you've held on to the belief that your life's problems have resulted from how your parents mistreated you. I get it. I felt the same way when I first started learning about these ideas. However, if you open your mind to it, you'll be able to see that there are certain patterns in your family system which can show where it all got screwed up. This will help you to see what you're up against and what changes need to be made so that your children won't yell at you for messing them up 20 years from now.

Seeing that your current issues go far beyond the mistakes of your parents, their parents, and the parents before them allows you to understand what's going on with you in a way that won't have you blaming anyone. Knowing that it's up to you to look at the ways your family has done things for generations can help you make important changes and heal your inner self. It can lead you to address the things you can change within yourself, instead of blaming other people for all of it. At some point, we must grow up and mature. We do this when we realize that our parents are flawed and so are we. Once we accept that, we can start to face and resolve our problems—many of which are similar to the problems our parents have. When you're willing to look, it's almost impossible to avoid seeing a connection between your parents' behavior growing up and your own behavior as an adult. It's all just too patterned and predictable to be ignored.

Looking Back to Move Forward

Our mothers and fathers grew up with a certain level of tolerance for upset, anxiety, disharmony, emotional connectedness, and demands from others. This all played out in their close relationships and was evidenced by their degree of reactivity to their children. Just like us, our parents, were unable to choose the cards they were dealt; they were subject to inherit the stuff of previous generations. The ability to deal with life circumstances, which is one of those things that gets inherited, can be referred to as emotional maturity—or, in Bowen's words, differentiation of self.

Through extensive empirical research, Bowen noticed patterns within families regarding the way individuals manage anxiety. This process takes people beyond blaming their parents to see the relationship forces at work that set them on their personal paths. Can you identify some of the patterns of relating to people that developed in your family, which have contributed to your current issues? To answer the question, think through the facts of your family relationship story; this can help you piece together some useful insights.

In order to simplify this process, allow me to show you a few examples of what I'm talking about. These are examples borrowed from Jenny Brown's book, which I mentioned earlier. The examples are designed to show the influence of various patterns that may develop between parents and children.

If you were the child your parents worried most about, you got accustomed to the emotional pattern of having them jump in to smooth out your difficulties. As a result, you probably instinctively expect and invite others to solve your problems. If one or both of your parents' anxieties were

projected onto you, it's likely that you got used to exagger-
ated criticism and correction. You might be prone to similar
negative overreactions. If one or both of your parents reduced
their tension by giving in to your demands, you may find it
difficult to let go of always feeling entitled. If one or both of
your parents confided in or leaned on you when things were
tough or distant in their marriage, you're likely to have an
easy time giving advice but a tough time accepting it. If you
were pushed to center stage by parents who got a sense of
security and esteem from applauding your achievements in an
exaggerated way, you likely can't tolerate not being important.

Do any of these patterns ring true for you? It's not neces-
sarily the case that our parents' ways of being have caused
us to have limitations. Instead, it makes sense to say that our
natural responses have been influenced by our parents, and
they were also influenced by family patterns that span back
several generations and will continue into future genera-
tions. Everyone's path to emotional maturity is different.
Knowing that we all have ways we react to the people we
love based on what we've inherited is a necessary step in
breaking that pattern. We must become more aware of the
automatic responses that relieve our stress. Because although
they are instincts we've inherited to make ourselves feel better
in the moment, they're not the responses that will help us
make meaningful changes in ourselves and our relationships.
Remind yourself of who you want to be in your moments of
stress, and try to respond in a more logical manner, rather than
in the ways that would be predicted based on the patterns in
your family of origin.

Becoming more of a self means letting go of the idea
that your parents are the cause of your problems. It means

realizing that, irrespective of where they came from, your problems are your own, and you are responsible for yourself. Even though we can't control our family history, we can always control what we do moving forward, and this will impact not only our lives, but future generations in our families also.

Summary

When problems arise in our lives, we tend to react by immediately trying to get rid of them and the feelings they bring. We try everything in our power to avoid experiencing even the slightest discomfort or pain. But when we avoid our problems and try to get rid of them immediately, we only make things worse for ourselves in the future. When certain feelings you want to escape come to the forefront of your experience, don't react by resorting to the same old behaviors. You might feel better in the moment, but there will always be consequences down the road. Once you open yourself up to all emotions, negative and positive, you leave room to see what is truly going on in your life and relationships. When you stop trying to avoid problems, and embrace them as part of life, you can truly feel alive. As Leonardo da Vinci said, "Learn how to see. Realize that everything connects to everything else."

Activity: Feeling It

When something comes up that upsets you, bothers you, or makes you feel uncomfortable, start exploring those feelings instead of trying to push them away. Simply be with whatever's upsetting you. You might not know why it upsets you or how you want to handle it—and that's okay. You don't have to do anything but be with the anger, pain, anxiety, or discomfort you're experiencing. Sit with it, become aware of it. Your body is trying to tell you something. Your emotions are letting you know that something isn't resonating with you. As I mentioned in this chapter, whenever something upsets me, I meditate, listen to relaxing music, or write. You can do whatever allows you to have some time with your negative feelings. I refer to them as negative, because we've been conditioned to see any unpleasant or unsettling feeling as negative; the truth is, these emotions can be gifts, inviting us to become more aware when something isn't right. Do what allows you to connect with yourself: take a walk, go to a yoga class, sit in a quiet room, or listen to music. Just be with your feelings, allow them to be present. You'll be amazed at how managing difficulties by just feeling and being with them strengthens you to take on challenges in the future. Give your feelings time to be with you. Deal with them on your own, without trying to fix anything.

_____

_____

_____

_____

_____

_____

_____

_____

CHAPTER 6

. . .

Prisoner of Love,
or Free to Love

Remember: despite how open, peaceful, and loving you
attempt to be, people can only meet you as deeply
as they've met themselves.

~ MATT KAHN

GET FRUSTRATED with how movies and fairytales portray romantic relationships. In movies, someone is always in need of saving and looking for someone else to do it. Once they find a person to love, they suddenly change and become a better person. Poof! All their problems disappear. Love can only change you temporarily, if at all. Once the initial excitement is gone, you'll go back to being who you were and feeling how you felt about yourself before the relationship. This is why it's important to have a solid sense of self before committing to a long-term relationship—learning what you like and don't like, and being true to yourself, not someone else. Without the self-knowledge required to define your own boundaries, likes, and dislikes, you won't feel complete. Without knowing what your boundaries are, you won't attract a person into your life who could live within those boundaries. You won't know how to define and stand up for your own beliefs. When you look for other people to complete you, you end up placing unrealistic expectations on them, expecting them to fill the gaps existing within you.

You Complete Me

If you're looking for a relationship to complete you, chances are you'll end up in a dissatisfying one with someone who feels incomplete also. The feeling of falling in love at the beginning of a relationship is really the experience of falling in love with an idea of yourself. You feel passion and excitement, and you view yourself and your partner in a positive light. That's because someone new is attracted to you and seeing all that is good in you; in turn, you only view all the good qualities in your partner. But as anyone who's been married knows, the love goggles eventually come off. And when they do, the person who could once do no wrong suddenly has a million flaws—and also has no problem pointing out your flaws, too. This leads to even greater disappointment, since you entered the relationship looking to that other person to complete you.

With society telling us we need love to be complete, how do we know what real marriages and romantic relationships look like? When we compare our actual relationships to the ones we see projected in the media, it's easy to feel like ours are falling short. Movies usually end just at the start of the characters' romantic relationships. And the coupled-up characters always appear to be experiencing bliss. Well, of course. The beginning is the exciting part! What the movies don't show is what happens during and after the couple's fights, when all the making up is over. They leave out what happens when the children are waking the couple up at all hours of the night, the dirty clothes are scattered all over the floor, and the pile of bills keep getting bigger. They don't show what happens when the stressors of life are at their height. Movies distort the image of a romantic relationship, setting an unattainable standard. They trick us into thinking that love is all it takes to change the playboy, turning him into a lifelong monogamous partner. The relationships and marriages portrayed by the media are unrealistic, working the angle that true love conquers all, is totally fulfilling, brings endless happiness, and involves zero conflict.

As people embrace the media's view of love, it's becoming more common for them to enter relationships and marriages based on a desire for happiness and personal fulfillment. When the initial romantic feelings fade, people think the love is gone; they become an emotional subway station, transferring from one relationship to the next. This can become very problematic, because it sets unrealistic expectations about sex, love, and relationship intimacy.

In real life, people who look to romantic relationships to make them feel complete end up half empty. Your true love story begins with you becoming full, responsible, and competent on your own. Maybe this doesn't sound romantic or sexy, but it will help you create more mature, fulfilling, and emotionally connected relationships. If you're relying on someone else to complete you, you're putting your emotions, life, self-worth, and happiness in someone else's hands. You're setting yourself up for disappointment. You're placing too many expectations on your partner, expecting him or her to bring you the happiness and fulfillment you should be creating for yourself. You might end up a serial dater who ends the relationship as soon as it gets complicated. Or, even worse, you might remain in abusive relationships, expecting that things will change if you only love hard enough. Relying on relationships for your contentment will have you feeling stuck. After all, how do you break up with someone who feels like a part of you? How do you detach when you believe that losing the relationship will make you fall apart? How do you stay connected when you take everything so personally?

Self-Full Love

Accept everything about yourself, I mean everything. You are you and that is the beginning and the end, no apologies, no regrets.

~ Clark Moustakas

Self-full people have relationships that are fulfilling and satisfying. They maintain solid boundaries and have a clear idea of who they are, so they don't allow their relationships to become draining or overwhelming. Happily-ever after begins with becoming aware of yourself and actions—and like all good things in life, getting it doesn't come easily. I'm not implying that you can't have your love story. You most definitely can. But be prepared for it not playing out exactly the way it does in the movies. The work you do on yourself will eventually bring you what you want in a relationship. Even if you're in a committed relationship now, you can still work on yourself—and trust me when I tell you that your partner and your relationship will benefit greatly from those efforts.

In order to have a successful relationship with another person, you need to be confident in who you are as an individual. You need a solid inner self that can only be changed from within, not from outside influences. Society and the media teach us something different—that we must give up parts of ourselves and conform to our partners' needs for the betterment of our relationships. We must ignore who we are to help the people around us. As people-pleasers, we hear this message loud and clear. It's louder than the inner voice that tells us what our beliefs, values, priorities, and standards are. Our true voice becomes a distant whisper, drowned out by what's being screamed from the rooftops about what love and relationships should look like. Our beliefs fade as we conform to others' standards of what we should be. Because of the lifelong programming you've had, your entire way of thinking about yourself, your relationships, and the concept of true love is tangled in a web of lies. Once your worldview changes to be more congruent with your motives, you can turn up the volume on your true self, rendering the demands of others and society a murmur in the background. You can act according to what's in alignment with your sense of self, instead of impulsively acting how you think you're supposed to act.

I once had a client named Kim who used to feel incomplete unless she was in a relationship. This was uncomfortable for her, because she was constantly compromising her values to create harmony in her relationship. It was hard for Kim to admit, but she probably would have done anything—apart from murdering someone—to keep her relationships going. She felt it was her responsibly to make her boyfriend happy and do anything to please him. Sounds awesome for him, right? Well, it actually doesn't work out well for anyone in the long run. This way of being in relationship was an exhausting and lonely losing battle for Kim, who always did all the caring, loving, and working in her relationships. She believed she had to work hard to be loved and accepted. Kim didn't think people could just love her for who she was. She believed she had to do what people said in order to win and maintain their love for her. Interestingly, Kim loved her family, friends, and partner unconditionally, despite their flaws, mistakes, and mess-ups. Growing up in a family in which she was only shown love when she made a significant accomplishment, Kim thought the only way to be loved was to be perfect or do something to deserve it. One way Kim tried to do this was by always making herself available to help the people in her life.

Along her journey toward self-fullness, Kim realized that help means giving people the freedom to learn to take better care of themselves. Her boyfriend became so dependent on her to care for him that he stopped doing things for himself or the relationship. She came to realize that he was never going to do anything different as long as she kept stepping in to fix his problems or finish the work he left undone. This realization changed Kim's life, prompting her to take a step back and start considering what she could do to change. She realized that her boyfriend had the capacity to complete his own work, but he wasn't going to do it if she got to it first.

As I've said throughout this book, it's helpful to change your ideas about what it means to be a loveable spouse, child, parent, family member, friend, or person in general. Your transition to becoming self-full will be aided by your keeping in mind that it isn't selfish to prioritize yourself, even when you're in a relationship. In fact, your positive changes will contribute to the health of your relationships. When you only act for other in your relationships, you not only hurt yourself but also the people you love, because you keep them from growing and experiencing life. All this does is leave you and your loved ones resentful, lost, and confused. At least, that's what happened for a lot of my clients—especially for Kim. Kim was so quick to take responsibility for other people and clean up their messes that she didn't have any experience managing her anxiety or letting people figure out their own issues. Kim would have been better served by knowing herself and recognizing her discomfort with others' discomfort. This would have helped her give her boyfriend a chance to be his own person and grow within their relationship, even if it wasn't easy.

Personally, I always thought that maybe if I did more, loved more, worked harder, and solved all the problems, everyone would be happy. If I responded in better ways and became better at problem solving, then I could fix everything, and everyone would be happy. Not! No matter how I responded and how much I tried, it just never worked. The problems kept getting bigger and harder to handle until I had to surrender and realize something needed to change about the way I was interacting with people. You aren't here to save the world and ignore your own needs. You can be kind and gentle with yourself, showing yourself the compassion you so often try to show to others. People can't flourish, realize their dreams, or become self-sufficient if you do too much for them. You truly become the kind of person other people look up to when you care for your needs and honor yourself first.

Some of the people in your life may lack the necessary skills to be in a fully fulfilling and committed relationship, no matter what you do. As Sherry Agrov says in her book, *Why Men Love Bitches*, "You can't take a skunk and dip it in perfume and hope it becomes a puppy. Eventually the perfume will wear off and you'll still have a skunk." If you make all the necessary changes and still find yourself having major issues in a relationship, it may be time to consider your options and look at the facts of the situation. The ultimate goal is the growth of your happiness and well-being. If communicated properly, people who really understand what you're working toward will show you they care about what makes you happy.

When Guilt Keeps You from Setting Necessary Boundaries in Your Relationships

People whose beliefs are motivated by guilt often fail to set necessary boundaries in their relationships. This guilt comes from believing that prioritizing oneself over others is wrong.

My client Kim reminded me of how powerful our beliefs and ideas are in determining how we identify ourselves. Kim told me that when she wants to speak up to certain people in her life, a stream of guilt-based commentary starts pouring in her mind saying, "Come on, be nice," or "Just say yes and do what they want," or "Is it really that out of your way?" Those thoughts try to convince her that she's doing the wrong thing if she doesn't comply with other people's requests. But she's really just trying to do the right thing for herself and her relationships. As an exercise, I asked Kim to write a letter to guilt as a way to manage her feelings around it. I had her do this in order to practice how she would set boundaries in her relationships, starting with her relationship to guilt. Here's what she wrote:

Dear Guilt,

You have found countless ways to make me feel like a bad person for not complying with others' every demand, even if it isn't something that I want to do. You burn within my gut when I say "no" to someone even when I know saying "no" is the right thing to do. You sometimes go as far as to convince me that I am a bad person, even when I know I am not. You have your way of wiggling into my life, you take control of my actions, and you allow me to comply with doing things for other people to please them instead of myself.

I am finally going to take a stand and begin to set boundaries in my relationships and that boundary setting starts with placing limits around you. You sometimes make me feel like I don't have a choice, when really I do. I have noticed by giving into you, I become resentful because I let people walk all over me. Somehow, I have been led to believe that I am only a good person if I do that. Guilt, I am not a mean person. I am actually a good person; you may never see that in me, and that is okay because that is your job. I just wanted to let you know that I cannot let you run my life decisions anymore. You are harming my relationships and my ability to be my own person. So, I apologize, but I will be ignoring you when you try to sneak your commentary in and I don't agree with you. I will be available to hear you out when I am in need of your opinion.

Like my client Kim, we can all benefit from recognizing the ways in which guilt tries to keep us trapped, preventing us from setting limits in our relationships and learning to better manage our anxiety instead of reacting to it in people-pleasing ways to relieve our discomfort. This is especially important because guilt will convince us that saying yes in order to please others is a good thing that doesn't need to be changed. The main intention behind feeling guilty is a good one—to do what we believe is right—but sometimes all it really does is damage our relationships and keep us from living with autonomy and integrity. People-pleasers are especially affected by feelings of guilt and a need to be needed. They feel responsible for other people's feelings and are compelled to do the right thing all the time. This feeds the urge to say yes, even when they really want to say no. Guilt can trick us into thinking we can successfully ignore our needs and take on other people's responsibilities; but after a while, those people will rely on us more and more, weighing us down.

Setting Boundaries

> *Maxim for life: You get treated in life the way you teach people to treat you.*
>
> ~ Wayne Dyer

It's important to be self-full enough to put boundaries in place and hold other people accountable for their decisions and actions. If you step in and take that responsibility, you'll quickly feel worn out, undervalued, and resentful. As Brené Brown states in *The Gifts of Imperfection*, "It's also impossible to practice compassion from a place of resentment. If we're going to practice acceptance and compassion, we need boundaries and accountability." Set boundaries in your most intimate relationships so that you can feel accepted, heard, and loved. Part of feeling connected to people is allowing them to truly see you and what you're all about. If you live to please everyone and don't speak your truth, you'll feel alone and invisible. And guess what? You'll have been the one who put on the invisibility cloak.

A big part of figuring out who you are is learning about your limits. Once you know what they are, you can set appropriate boundaries with other people. I know it's a very difficult thing to do at first. I once thought I would never be able to set boundaries. I believed that boundary setting was for people much stronger than I was. However, after I started to slowly set boundaries, it got easier over time. When I began to see the positive results in my relationships, I didn't want to stop placing boundaries. I was finally gaining something from my relationships, and it felt great. Below is some advice on how to build boundaries. Let this serve as a reference when you need to be reminded of this in your relationships.

How to Build Better Boundaries

Know your limits. You won't be able to set boundaries if you have no idea where you stand. One way to understand what your limits are is to start listening to what makes you feel uncomfortable and resentful. Those feelings offer hints about which boundaries to set with the people in your life.

Be firm. Maintaining boundaries sometimes requires having direct conversations with the people in your life. In your intimate relationships, in particular, you need to talk about what you accept and don't accept. It's important that you speak up and be firm about your boundaries, especially if they've been crossed or violated.

Know that you're worthy. Self-doubt will stop you from setting the boundaries you deserve. You might fear how the other person will respond if you set and stick to your boundaries, or you may believe that if you're firm about holding your boundaries, the other person will reject or leave you. I used to feel guilty speaking up or saying no to a family member. I always felt that I should be able to manage any situation and thought saying yes all the time made me the perfect sister, cousin, daughter, and friend. It didn't work. I burned out. Know that you deserve to have your own life and way of thinking. You are worthy and deserving of respect.

Change your role in your relationships. The role you play in your relationships keeps you engaging in people-pleasing behaviors with no boundaries. When you always play the role of caretaker, you hyper-focus on others, putting yourself last. It becomes normal for you to ignore your own needs. When you start setting boundaries, you might get some pushback from the people in your life who've come to have certain expectations of you. But you must remember that it's okay to set boundaries and change your role in your relationships. You can still be caring and loving, just not at your own expense.

Make time for yourself. Give yourself permission to prioritize caring for yourself. When you start putting yourself first, you'll become more motivated to set the proper boundaries, because you'll no longer want to accept what doesn't work for you. Making time for yourself includes understanding the importance of your feelings and valuing them just as much as you value others.

Apply the boundaries. It's one thing to talk about setting boundaries but quite another to actually apply them. We want people—especially our partners—to be mind readers, but that isn't realistic. In fact, that type of thinking will only get us into trouble. If someone has hurt you, it's important that you speak up about it in a calm, firm, and rational way. Most people think they only have two options: scream at the person who upset them, or stay quiet about it. But there's a third option. In a respectful way, tell the person what bothered you and how you can work together to address the issue. This is a life-long project, and it will never be perfected. Don't beat yourself up if you don't do it seamlessly every time.

Don't expect to become a master at setting boundaries overnight. I'd be lying if I told you that I have perfect boundaries in all my relationships and always perfectly communicate how I feel when I'm upset. It takes a lot of practice to communicate your boundaries, and just when you think you have it down, something new comes up that really challenges you. You don't have to do it all at once, setting boundaries with everyone at the same time. You can start small by setting boundaries with people you think will be more accepting, then work your way up to the more difficult people in your life. At first it takes strength to set boundaries, but over time and with practice, it can be mastered. This chapter concludes with an activity that will help with the process.

Summary

After food, water, and shelter, the quality of your relationships determines the quality of your life. When you begin your transformation, the people around you will be affected by your changes as well. If you continue on your path of people-pleasing, you'll continue to get the same unsatisfactory results in your relationships. Take responsibility for the role you play in your relationships, and use your voice to contribute to making those relationships balanced and mutually satisfying. Step out of your comfort zone. It takes courage to make changes and set boundaries. I think you know the choices that will be best for you; they're usually the more difficult ones. As American author Caroline Myss has said, "You don't need a wishbone. You need a backbone."

Remember that when it comes to certain people, you'll have to be the one to set boundaries, express yourself, and continue to speak up about what's okay and not okay with you. You are ultimately responsible for how you communicate and manage yourself in your relationships. Some people won't make it easy for you to do this, and your relationships with those people may always seem complicated. The process of speaking up and setting boundaries is more manageable when you don't try to change anyone and only focus on managing your own internal experience. I leave you with this bit of wisdom: The most difficult people will help you grow the most toward your self-full goals.

Activity: Setting Boundaries

You must change how you react to people before you can change how you interact with them."

~ Rick Kirschner

There's a saying that goes, "People who irritate us usually have something to show us about ourselves." This week, whenever someone irritates you, ask yourself: What is this person bringing out in me that I don't want to see? For example, when you're around a person who's always irresponsible, you might remember times when you've been irresponsible or have had to be more responsible to make up for another person's under-functioning. If it's a family member, close friend, or intimate partner who's challenging you, think about your own behavior in the relationship. Have you contributed to the situation by saying yes instead of no too many times? Have you failed to communicate that something was bothering you? Susan Fee, author of *Dealing with Difficult People: 83 Ways to Stay Calm, Composed, and in Control,* explains, "If you don't look at your own actions, you end up making the other person 100% of the problem."

Once you understand what triggered you and how you contributed to the situation, you can address the person in question. For the purposes of this activity, I would like you to confront someone this week who has crossed a boundary with you. Ideally, you'll choose a close friend, partner, or family member, because those are the people it's most important to address directly. If the person is an acquaintance or distant family member whom you only see everyone once in a while, it's probably not worth discussing.

Before you confront this person, prepare yourself. Ask yourself these questions: In what ways do I want this person's behavior to change? In what ways do I want my behaviors to change in relation to this person? What have I experienced, over time, from this relationship? It's important to set goals before you decide to speak to a person about what things you'd like to see change.

If you think the person will react negatively, try to plan your response in advance. For example, will you simply walk away? Say that you'll talk later when he/she is less upset? Take deep breaths until she/he relaxes? Choose whatever response works for you and your situation in that moment. Remember, you'll know you're becoming more self-full when facing issues head-on produces some anxiety. That uncomfortable feeling is part of the change process. Doing this work is guaranteed to make you anxious and uncomfortable; there's no way around it. But with some practice, that anxiety will subside. It's hard work to have fulfilling relationships, but it's worth it—and honestly, it's a lot harder to maintain relationships that aren't working.

CHAPTER 7

• • •

Moving Through Anxiety Finding Happiness, and Becoming Self-Reliant

Even if you're on the right track, you'll get run over if you just sit there.

~ WILL ROGERS

BUILDING SOMETHING, working toward our goals, and dealing with what needs to be dealt with in the moment all contribute to happiness. This emotion we call happiness can't be given to us, and it isn't something we create by instantly gratifying our urges in the moment. Respect, self-worth, and self-reliance—some of the elements that make up a person's happiness—can't be earned through avoidance behaviors either. When we're anxious, we become inadequately or excessively involved in others' lives. We use drugs, gamble, overeat, under-eat, shop, or work too much. We engage in avoidance behaviors to suppress our uncomfortable feelings instead of trying to manage our experiences and ourselves. Avoiding discomfort and sticking to what feels good is a surefire way to stay stuck and stunt your personal development.

People think that the anxiety and discomfort we experience in distressing situations is the main problem. It's not. That feeling like your back is up against the wall is an indication that there's a problem. It's the fire alarm, not the actual fire. In other words, anxiety is a symptom, not the actual disease. Anxiety is the sign that lets you know you aren't getting your fundamental needs met. It's the signal letting you know that you need a tune-up.

When we change our perspective to see anxiety not as a disease that needs curing, but as a symptom of the real problem, genuine change starts taking place. Instead of seeking to get rid of anxiety immediately, we're able to work with it, be with it, and understand it. If a fire alarm went off in your home, you might first asses the situation, look around, and try to identify the source of the smoke. You might call the fire station for backup if you see an actual fire. But I'm sure you wouldn't just run off and do nothing about it, hoping the fire would take care of itself. Similarly, if you were to feel a lump in your throat or breast, you probably wouldn't just assume it was benign and never get it checked out. That, however, is more or less what most of us do when we feel anxious. We do many things to avoid or run from our anxiety, instead of trying to check it out and see what it's telling us about our lives. We numb ourselves or cause harm to ourselves without investigating the real source of our suffering.

Millions of people are prescribed drugs like Xanax—a medication that research has shown to be more difficult and dangerous to withdraw from than heroin—to subdue their anxiety, often without any other treatment or further assessment of the problem. Studies have shown that while Xanax reduces anxiety in the first weeks of taking it, a reduced dose in an effort to stop use is associated with a worsening of anxiety by up to 350%. Today, estimates suggest that over 50 million prescriptions of Xanax and its generic formulations are filled in the US every year. This is how serious anxiety is and how much it affects people's lives.

There's something about the feeling of anxiety that makes people believe it's the problem. I can assume this is because it's so damn uncomfortable to be anxious. I get it. If I have a headache I take an Aleve. But if those headaches continue, there may be an underlying issue that I'm ignoring, and taking Aleve won't really solve anything. We treat anxiety like it's something unnatural that must be eradicated with medication. Some doctors, psychologists, psychiatrists, and pharmaceutical companies actively push the drug, which reinforces this belief. But in reality, that specific solution only increases the problem almost fourfold! I understand that some people really suffer from debilitating anxiety, and medication is a way for them to function in their daily lives. However, study after study has demonstrated that people who don't need the drug are being prescribed it. People who could learn to better manage their anxiety in other ways are popping Xanax instead of actually dealing with their lives. If you really want to get rid of chronic anxiety, you must get clear about how to manage yourself in stressful situations. Once you do this, the symptoms of your anxiety will actually start to reduce. The other solutions you attempt will likely only make the problem worse in the long run.

Biological Responses to Anxiety

There are three basic biological responses to anxiety: fight, flight, or freeze. These are our evolutionary go-to moves when a situation arises that makes us anxious. But what if instead of these three options we choose a different path? What if we choose to respond instead of react? Through our evolution over time, humans have developed the ability to logically think through situations instead of just react to them. Believe it or not, anxiety can decrease over time; but it can also continue, and even get worse, through the use of avoidance solutions like the ones listed above.

Some examples of reacting when anxiety arises are throwing a fit; running away from the situation by going to the casino, bar, or mall; turning on the TV; or getting in bed and taking a nap. By contrast, responding instead of reacting when anxiety arises includes recognizing the anxiety, accepting it, self-soothing by looking at the facts, and getting grounded in the present moment.

If you repress your feelings of anxiety, they can sometimes manifest as physical symptoms. They can keep you awake at night, deplete your bank account, or affect your close relationships. If you engage in harmful behaviors to repress anxious feelings, it's time to seek help in order to find healthier ways to cope. I once attended a conference at which the main speaker, a psychotherapist in practice for over 30 years, stated that every person who came into his office was displaying a unique attempt at managing anxiety. Instead of attempting to fix his clients, he simply tried to understand their problems from their perspective, making therapy a research effort rather than a problem-solving adventure. He stated, "The more uptight I am about trying to fix the problem, the worse the client does. The more I take a research stance, the better they do." As I stated in a previous chapter, this holds true for people in general: They do better when they aren't trying so hard to fix their problems and instead just get curious about what's going on with them. Be careful not to confuse that with ignoring or being in denial about the issue. Totally ignoring the issue is just as damaging as becoming overly involved in it or trying to fix it. Think about it. When you're drinking, using medication, watching too much TV, or overeating, how much of the attempt to avoid the problem actually gets in the way of you really solving it?

There are different reasons for your anxiety, including your genetics, temperament, how you grew up, your environment, what you eat, and a combination of these. However, the reasons you may be experiencing anxiety are personal to you. The limbic system—the personal alarm living in your brain—gets alerted whenever you're anxious. If you're having trouble managing your emotions to the point that you don't know if there's real danger, you're likely to experience chronic anxiety. However, it's important to remember that anxiety is a symptom, like an engine light coming on or an alarm sounding. Don't ignore it by throwing yourself into harmful behaviors. That's the easier, more temporary fix; it's hardly a solution for life. I know it's hard to change, but just remember, as psychologist Steven Hayes said, "If you always do what you've always done, you'll always get what you've always got."

Going from Anxious to Self-Reliant

Matthew came to see me after his anxiety started affecting his work, his functioning, and his personal relationships. He went as far as to fill a prescription for Xanax, because it's the way most of his family members dealt with anxiety. However, he was nervous to take it because of the side effects; he didn't want to suffer from weight gain, lose motivation, or become dependent on medication. Matthew explained that his cousin constantly has to increase her dose and can't even go on a long drive without taking a pill. Matthew was born into a hardworking family that made a comfortable living.

His father worked a lot while his mother stayed home to raise him and his sister. Matthew explained that his mother had always been very loving, to the point that she did everything for him. Even though he was in his 30s, she would buy his household essentials and check in on him weekly to make sure he had food in his fridge. She was always worrying about him and making sure he was okay. Just before coming to see me, Matthew lost his job. Unsure what to do next, he decided to move back in with his parents until he could find another job. Instead of feeling less anxious because he no longer had to worry about paying bills, Matthew felt more anxious than ever. He couldn't understand why.

If someone is always taking care of you and worrying about you, it's difficult for you to build a mature self. Like Matthew, it may lead you to lose a sense of agency and competency in your life. When Matthew moved in with his parents, he started engaging in compulsive online shopping as a way to manage his anxiety. He funneled all his energy into that behavior instead of taking the time off to develop self-awareness and decide what he wanted to do next. Matthew would use his mom's credit card to buy himself out of the uncomfortable experiences that, if he had confronted them, would actually have allowed him to develop clarity and self-confidence. Matthew was feeling unhappy, incompetent, immature, and irresponsible—especially after his mom saw the credit card bill. Instead of getting mad, she had him agree that they wouldn't tell his dad.

Matthew explained, "When I was younger, I thought that having financial stability and material wealth made people happy and self-confident. I mean, that's what society tells us. Money makes you happy, confident, and cool. In actuality, I have financial stability in my family but feel useless without a job. It made it worse that my mom didn't hold me accountable for my actions." What Matthew realized on his own is that when you don't have to work for what you have, it's hard to see its value. Self-confidence and self-reliance are built over time through our experiences; it's not something that can just be handed to us. If we aren't given the opportunity to manage our own difficulties or problems—because we're too busy buying our way out of it or engaging in avoidance behaviors—we'll never develop confidence in our abilities or ourselves. We'll always be anxious when new and challenging circumstances arise, which will have us repeating old patterns to get immediate relief.

After some time, Matthew decided to embrace his anxiety and work with it instead of avoid it. As he explained, "We don't grow without reaching outside our comfort zones." Self-confidence works just like the muscles in our bodies; it grows according to the amount of effort we put into building it up. If you avoid situations that challenge you, the muscle of your self-confidence will never develop or grow. The same is true for the people you help. When you constantly take over for them, you keep them from becoming capable, causing their self-confidence muscle to atrophy. The use it or lose it principle definitely applies here. Matthew was used to always getting what he wanted from his mom. He explained to me that when it came to finding a job, "I just wanted to get there already, without having to fill out applications and go on interviews." If you don't get comfortable with being uncomfortable and only live for instant gratification, you wont ever reach your goals. Matthew was able to sit with his discomfort and start working on finding a career instead of just another job. He moved out of his parents' house, got married, and bought his first home. Once Matthew stopped avoiding his discomfort, he was able to grow from it. This process of building self-confidence doesn't happen overnight, and it certainly isn't instantly gratifying. However, it does help us to better manage our lives and decrease the anxiety that can sometimes overwhelm us.

Bring Thinking to Emotions

Ask yourself this question: How many of my decisions are motivated by anxiety, and how many are well thought out? When I first asked myself that question and answered it honestly, I got a big wake up call. I realized that many of the decisions we all make in our daily lives are driven by anxiety and emotions. We take action to avoid feeling anxious or make decisions to reduce our discomfort. But in reality, those decisions can possibly lead to more discomfort down the road. When we make anxiety-based decisions, we aren't being true to what we really want. We act impulsively, inevitability causing us to experience more anxiety in our lives. It's a paradox if you think about it. We make decisions to try to reduce anxiety in the moment, only to find that it actually increases over time.

So what can we do about it? The first thing is to work on ourselves and realize it's not about what our anxiety wants, it's about what we want. Our anxiety stems from past experiences and can even be passed on from generation to generation. It's that twisted feeling you get in your gut telling you there's danger nearby. Sometimes it makes sense to listen to your anxiety about a situation, but most of the time it's just rubbish from the past. That's why it's important to add thinking to your emotions in the decision-making process. Ask yourself: Is this really something to be anxious about? What's the best decision I can make under the circumstances? When you bridge that gap between thinking and feeling, you stop bringing past anxieties into the present and start solidifying your sense of self. The real difficulty will be in keeping yourself from seeking a quick fix or hoping other people will solve your issues for you.

Love, Self-Respect and Self-Confidence

I once worked with a client who bought other people material things to make himself feel worthy of love. He used money as a way to obtain love and was on his fifth marriage as a result. In each marriage, he believed he could save his wife by taking her out of poverty and giving her what he saw as the good life. His main hobby was going to the casino with thousands of dollars in cash. He bought his sense of importance this way, through fleeting moments of happiness and instant gratification. People looked up to him at the casino, and his wives initially saw him as a savior; this is exactly what he wanted. He wanted to be respected and admired because he was wealthy—not because he was a good partner or a competent, responsible human being. Unfortunately, his gambling eventually turned into a serious addiction. He got hooked on the brief moments of pleasure his gambling gave him. Even more so, he became addicted to being admired by other people, even though it wasn't for his personal attributes or because he lived a life of value. Eventually, his friends and his wives saw beyond the money. When conflict arose in those relationships, he didn't know how to handle it, and things fell apart.

If you want close relationships and desire the experience of connection that comes from truly being respected, you have to build confidence within yourself, developing the capacity to manage yourself in conflict. Selfless, people-pleasing behaviors work against this, because they stem from a need to give or buy things in exchange for love. People-pleasers see love as a transaction—something that comes with a price tag—instead of being appreciative of who they are and what they have to offer. Happiness, love, and respect aren't waiting out there for you to get tomorrow or the next day, after you've gotten the promotion, won the lottery, lost the weight, or gotten married. Developing self-reliance is an inside job; it's not about covering up insecurities with material things and external approval. Life is always offering us opportunities to act in alignment with our values instead of acting to avoid things that trigger our insecurities, like challenging relationships or difficult tasks.

My client always looked to the outside world to provide him with security, love, confidence, and respect, because that's the only way he knew how to offer it to himself. He thought if he offered gifts, money, and financial security, the other stuff in his relationships would be easy. This made him extremely uncomfortable, but he hid that discomfort by constantly cycling through relationships. He used external situations and people to regulate his emotions. Living this way is like being on a rollercoaster ride that never ends—the ups and downs, highs and lows are intense and unrelenting. You can take control of your life and get uncomfortable now for a better reward later, or you can take the easy, more predictable route and be uncomfortable later with no end in sight. As my mother-in-law once said when my daughter was throwing a fit and I didn't react, "It's good you don't give in to the easier option. Cry now, or cry even harder later." People who can't regulate their feelings often look outside themselves for sources of soothing. When they become too anxious, too sad, or too easily triggered, they end up reaching for counterproductive ways to reduce their anxiety in the moment.

Being Self-Reliant

If you think about anything that has truly made you feel good about yourself, it probably involved working toward a goal. Good things—things of value—never come easy. As the saying goes, "There are no shortcuts to any place worth going." If a task were easy, it wouldn't help you see how competent you are. You must remember that you can meet, be with, and make it through anything. Over time you develop this confidence in yourself to overcome whatever challenges you face.

I recently had a conversation with one of the greatest thinkers I know: my 7-year-old niece. She's always pondering something and loves asking me questions about everything. Most of the time I don't have an answer for her and turn to Google to help give her a response. I've learned to do this, because if I ever make up an answer, she'll call me out by saying, "That doesn't make sense." The other day, she asked me, "Auntie, why do shots hurt?" I answered by saying, "They hurt because the doctor has to prick your arm with the needle to get the medicine inside." She answered, "Is there another way they can get you the medicine so you won't get sick that doesn't hurt?" I replied with, "I wish there was another way to give a shot, but that's the only way it works." She was quiet for a moment and then said, "Well, sometimes to get better or to not get sick, you have to go through pain." I answered, "Yes, that's very true." If you ever need a clear perspective on things, just talk to a kid.

Like my niece pointed out, anything worth working toward takes some hard work or struggle. There's no way around it! Trust me, I've seen people try. For example, no matter how many times gambling addicts go to the casino, their happiness is short-lived, especially when they're losing.

To overcome the addiction and find peace, they have to make concerted efforts—to go to treatment or support meetings, for example—and experience discomfort. In order to maintain their recovery when inevitable stressors come about, they have to learn different strategies to manage their anxiety. My grandfather used to say, "With hard work and sacrifice comes great reward." Self-confidence and courage don't come before accomplishing a difficult task; they're the result of working hard and getting the job done.

We all start out hesitant and a little fearful when approaching a challenging task that is of some consequence to our lives. But in order to get anywhere or achieve anything in life, we have to face our fears. As Nelson Mandela once said, "I learned that courage was not the absence of fear, but the triumph over it. The brave man is not he who does not feel afraid, but he who conquers that fear." When you start trying to change your unhelpful behavior patterns, you're going to experience some fear and doubt; but you have to learn to live with those emotions and manage them so you can keep moving forward toward your goals.

Becoming a confident person is a process of trial and error through which you make your own decisions based on who you want to be within each situation you face. This allows you to act for self and make your needs a priority. I started to develop confidence when I decided to think for myself and move forward with my decisions. As Cheryl Strayed says in her book, Brave Enough, "Nobody's going to do your life for you. Whether you're rich or poor, out of money or raking it in, the beneficiary of a ridiculous fortune or terrible injustice, you have to do life yourself. You have to do it no matter how unjust or sad your circumstances, no matter how hard it is. Self-pity is a dead-end road; it's up to you to drive down it or find an alternative route." What I learned, and what I want to share with you, is that if you want to become more self-full, you must first become more self-reliant. To reach the ultimate destination of self-full self-reliance, you've got to be willing to act for self and put in the work it takes to live a more fulfilling life.

You can't buy or please your way out of being human or having insecurities. I can't count the number of times I've heard people say things like, "If only I made more money. I would be happy." You can only purchase so much stuff, please so many people, and run away for so long until you reach a limit and can't do it anymore. Those behaviors will keep you working hard without much at all in return. Becoming self-full means working on tasks that build you up and reflect the truth about who you are. Would you rather spend your life avoiding pain or living with purpose?

What Society Says Should Make Us Happy

Sometimes situations arise that provoke negative feelings, which don't exactly match what society tells us we're supposed to feel. As humans, we're meaning-making beings. We all have daily experiences out of which we derive some meaning; most often they're based on what society has taught us. For example, when I was in my early 20s I thought there was something wrong with me because I didn't want to party every night. Society and my friends told me that's what you do in college and in your 20s, but it didn't make sense to me. I'd go out to a club only to be groped by sweaty guys, cringe at the super loud music, and pretend I was wasted. I'd wind up miserable and tired every time. I thought I was just a boring loser and believed there was something wrong with me.

That's how I interpreted those events, because the way

I felt didn't match what society was telling me. I weighed myself against the standard set for people my age within my culture and believed I was inferior as a result. I thought this revealed some truth about who I was. As I got older I came to realize that I'm the type of person who enjoys daytime actives and doesn't care for going out at night. Our cultural norms put pressure on us to fill certain roles. When our lives don't match society's expectations, we make the faulty assumption that there's something wrong with us. This is especially true when you don't have a strong sense of self. You get swept away by current fads and ideas about how you should live your life. When you define a self, you can evaluate trends and make your own decisions based on your values.

When your actions match your values, you feel more in control of your environment. Feeling this way contributes significantly to an overall sense of wellbeing. When what you do is in line with what you believe, your self-esteem and happiness grow. Even if you start taking more risks to act for self, you'll paradoxically feel less fear and anxiety. Having a sense of control in your inner world will make you less likely to experience hopelessness, helplessness, or depression. This, in turn, will make it easier for you to take on challenges. Life is not about what other people can do for you; it's about what you create, what you overcome, and what you aim to accomplish.

Learning to Deal with Your Outer and Inner Critics

People who change the world have declared independence from other people's expectations!

~ Unknown

One of the biggest factors that keeps us from being true to ourselves and reaching our potential is fear of criticism. When you struggle with people-pleasing behaviors, you essentially base all your actions on gaining other people's approval. Somewhere along the way you were led to believe that other people's approval gives you value as a person. Maybe your self-worth, self-esteem, and value are tied into being liked and accepted by other people. When this is the case, you believe your emotional health is contingent on the approval of others; in most cases, that's because you've given them that control over your life. You allow their actions to dictate your inner experience.

When you've handed over control of your life, any criticism of you, your work, or your decisions can be devastating. Because you've placed so much value on other people's opinions of your worth, they have the potential to destroy you. People-pleasers take criticism very personally—mainly because they can't separate themselves from their actions. Recognizing the difference between the person you are and the things you do is vital in the process of no longer devaluing yourself due to criticism from others. Once you stand for self and learn to manage your own emotions, your worth as a person won't be negated or degraded based on others' negative opinions of you. Not acting for self gives other people power over how you feel about yourself. As personal development writer Cynthia Kersey reminds us, "The negative comments of others merely reflect their limitations—not yours." The words people say speak more about them than they do about you. If you can keep that in mind the next time someone tries to criticize your life and your choices, you won't take their words to heart or make them mean anything about who you are as a person. Motivational speaker Zig Ziglar put it this way: "Other people and things can stop you temporarily. You are the only one who can do it permanently."

The worst kind of criticism is the kind you internalize and use against yourself, over and over again. I learned first-hand that the inner critic we all have inside of us can be the cruelest and most unforgiving. The negative narratives we tell ourselves about who we are prevent us from finding our purpose. They cause us to get stuck in jobs we hate, stay too long in relationships that aren't working, and conduct lives that generally lack meaning.

In my view, the inner critic is an echo of the voices of the meanest critics from our past—the teacher, parent, coach, or grandparent who said we couldn't do it. Their voices follow us as we get older and, over time, develop into our inner critic. As time goes on, that critic's voice becomes so loud that it doesn't allow us to chase our dreams, follow our purpose, or realize our true potential. I'm sure you've tried to get rid of that hateful voice by trying to ignore it or, perhaps, listening to what it has to say. Maybe you allow it to tell you who you are and what you're capable of accomplishing.

If you want to stop letting your inner critic defeat you, you first have to come to terms with the fact that the voice exists and understand that it doesn't speak the truth about who you are and what you can achieve. Critical voices may have you set unrealistic and impossible standards for yourself. Turn down the volume of your inner critic's voice by becoming aware that those thoughts are not your own; they are created from fear and anxiety. Sign a peace treaty with yourself and keep moving forward in pursuit of your goals. With every step forward and every accomplishment, the voices will get increasingly quieter until you don't hear them anymore. I think it's important to prove your inner and outer critics wrong. Show them that their words don't and won't speak the truth about who you are and what you can accomplish.

Your life is valuable, and you don't want to miss out on it because of what other people have to say. You may have dreams of becoming a teacher, nurse, doctor, musician, famous actor, or world's greatest mom or dad. Your goals are personal, and only you know what motivates you to get out of bed in the morning. As inspirational speaker Mastin Kipp said, "If you're waiting for the world or your circumstances to change first—you'll just keep yourself stuck." It's up to you and no one else to shut up those negative voices and go for whatever it is you want to try. Below are some summed up inspirational stories from Cynthia Kersey, the best-selling author of *Unstoppable: 45 Powerful Stories of Perseverance and Triumph from People Just Like You.*

Fashion photographer Richard Avedon tried to convince Cher that she didn't have the right look to be a model. He told her flat out, "You will never make the cover of Vogue because you don't have blond hair or blue eyes." When she did become a model, Vogue sold more copies than it had ever sold before.

When Gustave Leven was making plans to launch Perrier in the United States, several consulting firms advised him, "You're foolish to try to sell sparkling water in the land of Coca-Cola drinkers."

A New York publisher told James Michener, after reading his first unpublished manuscript, "You're a good editor with a promising future in the business. Why would you want to throw it all away to try to be a writer? I read your book. Frankly, it's not really that good." Michener's manuscript, titled *Tales of the South Pacific,* was eventually sold, later won a Pulitzer Prize, and went on to be adapted for stage and screen as *South Pacific.*

Those are just a few examples of people who were told

they couldn't do it and then did. It's always hard to be criticized, especially when the critic is someone in a position of power. Maybe the critics were well-intentioned and only trying to be realistic. I, for one, am happy I didn't listen to the high school teacher who told me only 1% of Americans get Ph.D.'s., and even if I got into graduate school for my doctorate, I'd have a hard time completing it, since most Ph.D. programs average a 30% completion rate. She was trying to lead me toward career choices that she thought would be more suitable for my test scores and grades. Her voice followed me all the way through my academic career, discouraging me but also pushing me.

When it comes to chasing my dreams, there's nothing I love more than proving people wrong. I worked hard and made a lot of sacrifices, but now I can live the rest of my life as a therapist and professor, helping others live to their potential. There's an African Proverb that states, "When there is no enemy within, the enemies outside cannot hurt you." It's always going to be a bit of a struggle, but I'm grateful every day for never letting my inner and outer critics tell me who I am or what I can become. I wish the same for you.

Confident in Your Decisions

Even if you have financial means, you need to budget and live within a certain income—otherwise, the money could disappear very quickly. A good example of this is the average professional athlete in the U.S., who makes more in one season than most Americans make their entire careers. Statistics show that 78% of NFL players and 60% of NBA players file for bankruptcy within five years of retiring. Most of this is due to incompetence and poor planning. People aren't usually trained in budgeting, the tax system, or long-term financial planning. Knowing this, I realized I had a big job ahead of me when I became executor of my aunt's estate. Not only was I tasked with managing her children's financials, I also had to learn how to manage my stress and anxiety whenever they came to me asking for something that wasn't in their budget. As an executer, I had to learn to say the word I was most afraid of saying: no. If that wasn't enough, I had to learn to say it to people who had never heard the word in their entire lives. But the reality is that trustees who aim to please beneficiaries will have them run out of money as fast as a professional athlete.

I was in a real dilemma. If I said yes to the beneficiaries in an effort to please them, they'd be happy in the moment; but if I allowed them to spend all their inheritance, they wouldn't be very happy in the long run. Everything I believed about what it means to be a good, helpful person changed when I was put in this difficult position. I recognized that if I stuck to my usual people-pleasing ways, my cousins would suffer by losing their inheritance. I really didn't have much choice but to stand up for my values and do what I knew was right, which was to make sure my family members lived within their means and didn't overspend—to live according to my values and say no when it was necessary. I then had to find a way to teach them money management skills and show them how the process works so they wouldn't be dependent on me their entire lives. This way they could one day step up and function more independently.

With this as my ultimate goal, I first set out to work on myself and address my people-pleasing issues. I had to learn how to deal with confrontation and tell people things that might displease them. I had to finally stand up for my beliefs and be guided by my own values and principals. I am now thankful every day for this opportunity life gave me to grow and change. It provided me with the motivation to challenge myself and work on my issues. I used that experience to change into a more confident and self-reliant person. It taught me that the only way to develop independence is to work through tough situations by managing our anxiety instead of seeking an easy escape. By doing what makes us anxious, we learn to manage ourselves in uncomfortable situations, developing the strength to more effectively deal with difficulties in the future.

Through my process of becoming self-reliant, I learned some very valuable lessons that I'd like to share with you:

- People can learn to do things for themselves if you give them a chance to.

- If you're going to confront someone, wait until you've calmed down and can express yourself in a rational way.

- Do your part in your relationship and lend a hand to others, but not by doing things for them.

- Accept people for who they are, even if you don't agree with their decisions.

- When you're upset with someone, look at the part you played in the conflict—not to take the blame, but to take responsibility for yourself.

- Try to genuinely listen to others—not to come up with a response, but to truly hear what they have to say.

- Notice when you get the impulse to overly involve yourself in others' lives. When you feel it, resist the urge and occupy yourself with something else.

- When you have to tell someone disappointing news, stick to the facts. Leading with your emotions will only make things worse.

To become who you've always wanted to be and do what you've always wanted to do, you'll need courage. Getting rid of anxiety won't help you accomplish your goals; you'll do it by embracing fear, knowing it's scary to go for what you truly want, and doing it anyway. That's where bravery and courage come from. So, ask yourself the tough questions: What would I do if I weren't anxious? How would I act if I knew I had nothing to lose? Then take action and enjoy what it feels like to truly be free.

Summary

I use the terms *self-reliance* and *happiness* interchangeably, because I don't think you can have one without the other—at least not in the long run, anyway. Relying on others all the time—or, conversely, taking responsibility for others and neglecting yourself—doesn't make for a comfortable life. I think I first realized this when my aunt killed herself six months after my grandfather passed away. He thought he was doing right by always giving in and supporting her, but she literally couldn't live without him after he passed. So, in reality, his constant emotional support played a part in her early demise. That was never his intention, of course, but it was the outcome of her life. The meaning I made of her death gave me the strength to make necessary changes in my life. If I constantly lived for others and took their responsibilities on as my own, I would lose and they would, too. If I didn't allow them to fall and learn to pick themselves up, I'd be robbing them of an opportunity to attain happiness. And if something were to happen to me, what would happen to them?

Life is meant to be challenging. If you attempt to run away from discomfort, you just end up cheating yourself and guaranteeing that you'll eventually fall even harder down the road. The good news is that in order to be happy and fulfilled, you just need to have your own back and be confident in your skills and abilities. As you become more self-full, you'll know that when a challenge arises—and, of course, it eventually will—you'll have all the necessary equipment to get through it. That equipment takes time to gather, and as anyone who lives in Florida knows, you can't scramble to the store on the day of the storm and expect to get everything you need to be prepared.

People aren't born with self-reliance; we gain it through a process of trial and error as we go through life making decisions. People who act with self-reliance feel more in control of their environment, which improves their overall sense of wellbeing. When what you do is in line with what you believe, your self-esteem and happiness grow. You can experience life the way you want to. Even though it often means taking more risks, it tends to be a far less fear-inducing and anxiety-provoking way of life. That's because being self-reliant means doing things for yourself. The more you do for yourself, the better you feel; the better you feel, the more confident you'll become.

Activity: Developing Self-Reliance

With this activity, I'd like you to take on a task that you've been scared to do out of fear of failure. Maybe it's starting that blog you always wanted to start, asking out that person you haven't had the confidence to ask out, interviewing for that job you want, or confronting someone who upset you. This week, do that thing you've been too afraid to do. Apply to that school, end that relationship, finish that book, say no—whatever it is, do it! And watch how it plays out. As director and author Benjamin Mee said, "You know, sometimes all you need is twenty seconds of insane courage. Just literally twenty seconds of just embarrassing bravery. And I promise you, something great will come of it." Use that courage and go get what you want, or at least get started on it. As I've been saying throughout this book, you don't get rid of anxiety about a situation by running away from it; you start to better manage your anxiety by placing yourself in situations that provoke it.

_____

_____

_____

_____

_____

_____

_____

_____

_____

CHAPTER 8

. . .

The Path To Becoming
Self-fullfilled

*Everyone thinks of changing the world, but no one
thinks of changing himself.*

~ LEO TOLSTOY

A S I'VE BEEN SAYING, trying to break the people-pleasing
pattern is difficult. You not only have to change your
response to other people, you also have to deal with their
changes in response to you. It's possible that in this process
of change, you'll become aware that your eagerness to please
stemmed as much from a desire to avoid hurting people's
feelings as it did from an unwillingness to deal with their
reaction to you. When the people in your life are accustomed
to you being in a certain role, they'll struggle to accept your
efforts to assume a different position. Their reactions are likely
to make you feel uneasy, allowing you to become aware of
why you were pleasing in the first place.

Stay strong by remembering that if you don't start to
make the necessary changes, you'll continue on the path
you're already on, which doesn't allow you to have fulfill-
ing relationships. Taking initiative in your life is more than

just professing that you're going to make changes; you must
be determined to build a strong sense of self and challenge
every bad feeling that stops you from saying no to the things
you don't want to do. You might start to feel angry once
you realize the degree to which people are resentful of your
changes, and it's possible you'll feel underappreciated, given
all you've done for them. Your feelings have been buried for
so long that they're likely to come up quickly as soon as you
start making changes. It's like opening a Coke bottle after
giving it a hard shake. Everything that was bottled up starts
fizzing, flowing out. The anger can come especially intensely
when others start to protest the changes you want to make
for yourself. However, you can wait and choose a different
response, other than the one your anger will produce. Imagine
what would be possible if you could independently sort out
your emotions before responding to a given situation. When
you've shaken up a Coke bottle, you can avoid the fizzy over-
flow by waiting a minute for the pressure to dissolve before
twisting the cap open. Similarly, you can allow the pressure
and intensity of your emotions to subside before you respond.
This doesn't mean repressing your emotions; it just means
giving yourself some time to equalize the pressure so you can
communicate your thoughts in a calmer mindset. You'll get
much more clarity than chaos—much more soda than fizz—if
you just wait a little bit.

When you live a selfless life, it feels natural to please
others and wrong to say no, so you wind up doing things
for other people in a rather automatic, impulsive fashion. At
first, going against the urge to do something for another will
feel strange and uncomfortable—almost unnatural. That's
because you know the other person will be dissatisfied with
your response to them. And this kind of reaction is something

you're unaccustomed to—after all, your objective your entire life has been to please. To suddenly stop aiming to please others will go against your original belief system about what it means to be a responsible person. It took me a while to get comfortable with the idea of displeasing others. It probably would have been almost impossible for me to change if my circumstances didn't force me to tell people things they didn't want to hear. At some point on your journey to self-fullness, you'll have to say something that someone else will have a hard time swallowing. The person may initially be displeased with your new responses, which might make you feel guilty or angry. But if you want to be free, once and for all, from your people-pleasing ways, you mustn't listen to guilt or anger. Claiming your freedom won't be easy, but I promise it will be well worth it.

As I mentioned, when my aunt passed away and I became executor of her estate, I was in charge of dispersing the money left to her two children. Her parenting policy was to give her children whatever they wanted, because she didn't want them to feel the temporary dissatisfaction of wanting something and not getting it. But once my grandfather passed away, consumed with pain, she spent a lot of her money in a short period of time. As a result, her children received less then they expected and it was difficult for them to comprehend the idea of changing their lifestyles.

Even if I wanted to, I couldn't say yes to their requests; there just wasn't enough money for them to have everything they wanted. As a lifelong people-pleaser, I found myself in an awkward position. I had to practice saying no with a group of young adults who'd never heard that word before. This was a big challenge for me. They got upset with me, and I, in turn, let guilt and anger convince me that I wasn't doing the right thing. I interpreted it as confirmation that saying no was a bad thing—but in reality, it was precisely the right thing to do. Giving in isn't the loving thing to do; it's the easier thing to do in the moment. After a while I started to get used to my family members lashing out at me. I started to take it less personally and realized that it made sense for them to get upset; after all, they weren't used to being told no. They were projecting their anxiety onto me, but I didn't have to internalize their emotions like I had in the past. Instead of lashing out or being overly apologetic, I stuck to the facts of the situation and explained what could and could not be done under the circumstances. This helped me remain calm and, to my surprise, actually relaxed them as well.

Charlotte's Story

My client Charlotte hated confrontation so much that in her ongoing efforts to avoid it, she failed to have a life of her own. Most of the time she felt miserable, and when she came to see me she had the sense that the way she'd been living had been misguided. Charlotte always thought she was doing right by the people in her life, but instead she wound up limiting herself and everyone around her. Through her experience in therapy, she came to realize that people need to be responsible for regulating their own emotions—a process called self-soothing. After spending so much of her life feeling responsible for others' feelings and carrying the heavy emotional burden of their mistakes, it was a profound experience for Charlotte to realize that she didn't need to do this anymore. As she explained during one of our sessions, "People need to clean up their own messes, especially when they're the ones who made the mess in the first place. I keep my life a certain way and follow the rules because I know that actions have consequences. People throw their crap around and then call me when it's just too much to clean up on their own. I have to allow them to figure it out on their own or they'll continue to run to me with every little problem."

Just like Charlotte pointed out, why would anyone in your life ever change if you continue doing the dirty work for them? Why would they learn or grow if you're going to take care of everything? Doing too much for other people just perpetuates their lack of responsibility. You play a part in losing yourself by taking on more than you need to. Of course, they play a part in the relationship dynamics too; but like I said, you're only in control of you. When you take on someone else's problems, your anxiety increases, and the other person is relieved for that moment. You're like an anxiety pill that takes away others' anxiety for a short period of time. But since anxiety is a natural part of life, it always comes back. The biggest problem is that the people taking the pill eventually get worse, because they aren't learning from the experiences that make them anxious in the first place. People can never get rid of anxiety once and for all; instead they have to practice managing it so they can build their resilience. This is exactly what Charlotte learned to do. She no longer wanted to prevent her family from developing tolerance and resilience to life's normal circumstances by trying to manage their challenges for them. She also realized that she had to learn to better manage herself and her uneasiness with confrontation. Charlotte put on her big girl pants and had some tough conversations with the people in her life in order to build her sense of self. Doing this created instrumental changes for her, as well as for her family members, allowing them all to lead more productive and fulfilling lives.

Other People's Problems Are
Not Your Problem

At an early age, you probably decided that other people's problems were your responsibility to fix. Wow, what a huge emotional burden! No wonder you feel exhausted and drained all the time. You invest so much energy into others, there's barely any left for you. Once you realize you're only responsible for yourself, your decisions, and your personal issues, you'll experience tremendous relief. Whenever someone asked Charlotte to solve something for them, she started telling herself, "It's not my problem." You see, there's a difference between having empathy for someone and losing yourself in the process of helping them. It's okay to be empathic and offer support, so long as you maintain your integrity in the process. That's what it means to be self-full. When you act selflessly, on the other hand, you relieve other people's anxiety by making their problems your own. You try to be the problem-solver for issues that aren't your responsibility to solve. Furthermore, you make it so that other people start expecting you to take away their anxiety. In essence, you become their emotional dumpster.

There are countless examples of how I've taken on other people's tasks and complications, especially within my family. For example, there was the time I had four pets, three of which came from a family member who no longer wanted to take responsibility for them. Thinking it was on my shoulders, I took them in and gave them a home. I never personally wanted to take care of more than one animal at a time, because I knew multiple pets would mean a lot more financial duties, time, and messes. However, I felt like I couldn't say no. I love having animals, but too much of anything can be overwhelming. What I should have told the original owners is that since those were their pets, they were responsible for either keeping them or finding them a new home. Instead, I took on their responsibilities and the stress that came along with them. I became angry and resentful toward the pets' former owners, especially during those times when taking care of the animals overwhelmed me. I realized that this wasn't a very helpful way to go about things. After some time passed, I had an honest and direct conversation with my family members, letting them know I was overwhelmed and needed some help with all the animals. Once I was open and authentic with them, they showed understanding and came up with a plan that worked for all of us.

Stuck in a People-Pleasing Pattern? Neuroscience Can Help

Currently, you're stuck in a certain pattern of interaction with the people in your life that keeps you in the people-pleaser role. As I'm sure you've already discovered—and as I've repeated many times throughout this book—it might feel impossible to break the people-pleasing pattern in certain relationships. You might have convinced yourself that you'll always be acting for others, and that your relationships with people will always be one-sided. You might think that your need to please somehow reflects the foundation of your rela-tionships and the truth about who you are as a person. Living selflessly will allow you believe that you have certain inherent flaws and negative qualities that are fixed and unchangeable. But it's important for you to understand and remember that how you identify yourself isn't permanent, because your ideas about who you are can change by you working on your perceptions, beliefs, and relationships. The notion that you can't change because you've always been a certain way just simply isn't true. You can change your behaviors, and your relationships can change as a result.

It's helpful to understand that your behaviors develop within the context of your relationships; they don't always reflect an internal issue or mental health problem. Thinking, "Well, that's just who I am. I can't change" is untrue and limiting in nature. Our context is part of us; it's an integral aspect of how we behave and react. However, it doesn't define us. Your context—which includes your family, friends, upbringing, culture, etc.—has led you to believe that making others a priority is a good idea. As a people-pleaser, that's just how your relationships have always played out. You have an automatic response to place other people's needs before your own. But although your past and context have impacted the way you think, act, and feel, it's possible for you to do things differently.

How we choose to respond to the people and circumstances in our lives gives us a sense of who we are. But we always have the opportunity to rebuild our sense of self and respond to situations differently in the future. If your relationships aren't working for you, change them. I'm going to explain to you some of the latest research from the field of neuroscience, which shows that our brains actually change when we change our minds, behaviors, and beliefs over time. This is great news! You aren't bound by the past, and you can certainly change your present and future. As science columnist Sharon Begley tells us, "Like sand on a beach, the brain bears the footprints of the decisions we have made, the skills we have learned, the actions we have taken. But there are also hints that mind-sculpting can occur." This means that our brains can change when we change the way we use them, even if we've done things a certain way for a long time. In other words, you aren't trapped being the person you've always been. You have the ability to change, and neuroscience research proves this. In the next section, I summarize some important research to help clarify the impact that changing your thoughts, behaviors, and beliefs can have on your brain. If you aren't a science nerd like I am, no worries; you can skip this section and go on to read the summary.

Neuroscience Research Shows That Change Is Possible

For decades, the dominant view of neuroscience was that the brain is a fixed entity, hardwired to be the same for our entire lives. Being that conventional neuroscience held the belief that the adult brain is hardwired, and no new neurons develop during adulthood, the expectation was that once the brain forms, people stay relatively the same over the lifespan. Some researchers have attempted to counter this idea by explaining that a person's mind influences the brain and how it operates. Neuroscientists like Jeffery M. Schwartz and Sharon Begley, authors of the book *The Mind & The Brain: Neuroplasticity and the Power of Mental Force*, challenge the idea that our brains are hardwired and claim that brain processes alone can't account for the full range of mental capacity, such as conscious free will. They argue that "mentalistic variables must be considered to reach correct understanding of the neurophysiological basis of behavior in humans." Through experiments conducted in the last decade, researchers have demonstrated that the mind has the power to shape the brain. This fascinating research shows the brain's ability to be rewired throughout the lifespan, challenging the idea that we're unchangeable once we reach adulthood. In other words, no matter how old we are, we can still change.

Brain Research

The findings of research conducted by Neuroscientist Mario Beauregard suggest that mental processes causally influence brain plasticity and brain functioning. According to Beauregard, "Indeed, by changing our mind we are changing our brain." This has been demonstrated through the neuroimaging studies Beauregard reviewed, which show that beliefs and expectations can clearly alter neurophysiological and neurochemical activity in the areas of the brain that express perception, pain, and emotions.

Neuroscientist Jeffery Schwartz made a fascinating finding when he was working with clients diagnosed with obsessive-compulsive disorder (OCD). When Schwartz had his patients focus their attention on their own positive behaviors rather than negative ones, he identified significant changes in their neural pathways. Encouraged by these findings, Schwartz continued to investigate the mind's ability to shape the brain. He did this through his own research and case studies of people diagnosed with OCD and depression. Schwartz used Positron Emission Tomography (PET) scans to measure metabolic activity in his patients' brains before and after a group therapy setting during which patients were told they were not the ones manifesting their obsessive thoughts; rather, their OCD was doing it. He also helped them respond to their OCD in a different way, emphasizing that their ways of responding to it could actually change their brains. Schwartz explains, "By refusing to accept obsessive thoughts and compulsive urges at face value, and instead recognizing that they are inherently false and misleading, the patients took the first step toward recovery." In a series of group therapy sessions, Schwartz had his patients stand up to OCD by telling them that their obsessive thoughts were "toxic waste from their brain;" he then had them focus their attention on positive things they like to do.

When looking at the PET scans after treatment, Schwartz found that therapy had altered the metabolism of the OCD circuit. As he explained it, "The changes we detected on PET scans were the kind that neuropsychiatrists might see in patients being treated with powerful mind-altering drugs." The patients who participated in Schwartz's research found that their obsessive thoughts became less intense, and they were able to replace bad habits with healthier ones, literally reprogramming their brains. Based on the extensive research he conducted, Schwartz concluded, "It is the brain's astonishing power to learn and unlearn, to adapt and change, to carry with it the inscriptions of our experiences, that allows us to throw off the shackles of biological materialism, for it is the life we lead that creates the brain we have."

Neuroscientist Sharon Begley also writes about how new science and the teachings of Buddhism work together to demonstrate the power we have to change our brains by changing our minds. She refers to experiments on neuroplasticity that have revealed the brain's remarkable ability to adapt and heal following trauma. As it turns out, the brain can even compensate for disabilities. She explains, "These breakthroughs show that it is possible to reset our happiness meter, regain the use of limbs disabled by stroke, train the mind to break cycles of depression and OCD, and reverse age-related changes in the brain." This coincides with the Buddhist belief that the mind has the ability to transform the self. Buddhists believe that negative thoughts in the untrained mind can go wild, triggering destructive emotions. The Buddhist practice of mental training helps individuals control their emotions and come to new understandings. Buddhist meditation, the ultimate form of mental training, allows individuals to transform their internal experience, no matter what's happening on the outside.

Neuroscientist Helen Mayberg conducted a study which revealed that antidepressants and placebos have exactly the same effect on the brains of people diagnosed with depression. Begley found the same results: "In patients who recover, whether their treatment consisted of one of the widely prescribed selective serotonin reuptake inhibitors (SSRIs) such as Paxil or a placebo that they *thought* was an antidepressant, brain activity changed in the same way." This suggests that the conscious beliefs held by depressed patients about their recovery are just as potent as medication in changing their brain chemistry. It's also a powerful testament to our capacity to change based on our beliefs.

Begley sums up the conclusions of numerous neuroscience studies by saying, "The conscious act of thinking about one's thoughts in a different way changes the very brain circuits that do that thinking." She also explains that these types of changes in the brain require focus, training, and effort. According to Begley, neuroimaging studies show that these changes are not only legitimate, they're generated from within the brain itself. She talks about it this way: "As discoveries of neuroplasticity and this self-directed neuroplasticity trickle down to clinics and schools and plain old living rooms, the ability to willfully change the brain will become a central part of our lives-and our understanding of what it means to be human."

Neuroscience research offers sufficient evidence of the mind's ability to change the brain, which indicates the extraordinary potential we have to change. I hope this paradigm shift can help you transform your understanding of the human mind and solidify the importance of making an effort to create changes in your life. As Thomas Lewis, Fari Amini and Richard Lannon, assert in their book *A General Theory of Love*, "In the end, all such discovery has one purpose: to help people reach their potential for fulfillment and joy. While we cannot alter the nature of love, we can choose to defy its dictates or thrive within its walls."

Summary

When you change how you think about who you are and the person you want to be in your relationships, your brain will change over time as a function of your new way of being. Neuroscience research shows that you aren't doomed to continue repeating the same patterns that have been making you unhappy. You can choose to make changes in your life, and you're capable of doing so. We must actively change our perceptions of who we think we are, so we can live the truth of who we really want to be. When you start consistently living in a self-full manner, you'll change, and the people in your life will, too. Some situations will pull you back into old patterns, and that's okay. It takes time for your neurons to wire together and result in new behaviors. At first, your changes in response to people will be a conscious, sometimes difficult and effortful process. This was certainly true for my client Janet. Her younger sister was very good at manipulating her into resuming old patterns of helping. It was difficult for her to say no to her sister, and at first it felt almost impossible for her to even utter that word. Even when she managed to say no, it somehow always ended up turning into a yes. It physically pained Janet to see her sister anxious, angry, or upset. That would lead to feelings of guilt and anger, which would pull her back into doing things for her sister that she knew wouldn't be helpful in the long run. However, over time and with consistent effort, it got easier for her to say no. Her sister's attempts at manipulating her stopped, because it was no longer serving either of them. Janet explained her changes to her sister this way: "That's your responsibly to take care of. If you need help, I'm available at these times. However, I won't do it for you." This will happen for you, too. Your new responses will ultimately generate different responses from the people in your life, which will allow you to enjoy smoother communication and improved relationships. By learning to set boundaries with her sister, Janet's relationship flourished, and both women experienced significant emotional benefits from the change.

If you've ever wondered if people can change, the answer is yes. Even people you never thought would change will surprise you by doing so once you start making more authentic and mature choices in the ways you respond to people. You just have to want it enough and realize that it's necessary for a better life. You do this by practicing self-fullness and becoming mindful of your responses to others, sitting with your initial discomfort knowing a better life is just around the corner. Once you do this, you'll no longer be the people-pleaser everyone takes advantage of, who doesn't have a sense of self. You'll be the person they respect—the one who's clear about what's okay and not okay. You won't be resentful anymore, and you'll get to enjoy open and honest relationships with the people in your life.

Activity: Becoming Self-Full

Reflect on this: What difference would it make if you tried to understand the role you've played in your relationships, and how would it benefit you to change that role? People tend to concern themselves with external things they can't control, when instead they should be looking within. Spend some time looking within, and decide what role you want to play as a family member, friend, employee, or person in general. Who is it you want to be in relation to others? After you decide this, use your life experiences as a way to practice being the person you'd like to be. The only way to do this is by being with others, exploring new ways of relating to them. Whenever possible, ask yourself: How can I change my response in this situation, without taking blame? How can I act more for self?

Every time Janet's sister asked her for something, Janet used it as an opportunity to practice responding differently. She treated each of her sister's requests like a dress rehearsal, preparing herself for the live performance of living as the person she wanted to be. Janet wanted to be a kind, understanding, and supportive sister, not a bossy and judgmental pseudo-parent. However, in order to do this, she had to change her response to her sister, regardless of how her sister behaved. Janet's sister gave her ample opportunities to work on changing in response to her. Janet used these times to practice patience and understanding. Now they have a relationship that feels more like a close sisterly bond between equals, instead of a distant and combative power struggle. Once Janet's sister felt less judged and more understood, she eased up on the demands she made of her.

CHAPTER 9

· · ·

Acceptance of Self

Nothing ever goes away until it has taught us
what we need to know

~ PEMA CHODRON

STARTED MAKING THE NECESSARY CHANGES to become more self-full when I realized that I was deeply depressed. At that point in my life, I felt lost. I experienced a constant sense of emptiness and had no passion for life. That's how serious people-pleasing is; that's why it's so important to change. But the truth is, it's hard to change when you think it's up to everyone else to do things differently. It can make you feel helpless, like your life and fate are out of your hands. For me, all the negative feelings I was experiencing perpetuated a greater need to please, which led to more disappointment and kept in motion the vicious cycle of blaming others for my misery. As I mentioned before, I started people-pleasing as a way to avoid dealing with my own life, gain others' acceptance, and manage my fear of criticism and disapproval. It was easier for me to place everyone's needs before my own so I wouldn't have to deal with discomfort. Eventually, people-pleasing became my automatic setting.

Pleasing behaviors usually start as a way for us to feel less anxious about our lives. We need to feel needed so we can prove to ourselves and others that we're worthy. We make ourselves indispensable so we wont be abandoned, rejected, or put down. We borrow a sense of superiority from others that feels good for a while but eventually becomes overwhelming. When I became more knowledgeable about Bowen Family Systems Theory, I finally got off my high horse and came back down to earth, truly humbled by what I'd learned. Having a sense of entitlement and thinking I was always right was no longer working for me or my relationships. Over time, I realized that the best way to improve all my relationships was to improve myself, my mind, and my actions.

For a long time, I ignored what depression was trying to tell me by keeping myself busy with other people's stuff. But once I stopped trying to protect myself from being depressed or anxious and tried to learn from those feelings instead, my life changed dramatically. I realized that depression was showing me my life wasn't congruent with what I wanted for myself. Though I knew I wanted more for my life, I felt stuck. I had no idea how to make the changes I needed for a better life, especially since I'd always sought relief by trying to fix other people's problems. Finally, I started to look within and ask myself, what advice would I give to someone with the same issues? The answers were readily apparent to me. I'd tell them to invest in themselves for once, instead of getting lost in everyone else's issues. I never saw myself as the one who needed help or needed to change; but after blaming others for so long, I had no choice but to take a hard look at myself. We're conditioned to think that if only other people would change, we'd be able to get on with a happier life. I thought if I just avoided my difficult family members, perhaps I could reach my potential. But, of course, that wasn't true. It was time for me to learn the lessons my own circumstances were trying to teach me. As Jenny Brown, MSW says in her book, *Growing Yourself Up: How to Bring Your Best To All Of Life's Relationships*, "Genuine maturity for life starts with learning to observe ourselves in our relationships, and appreciating that problems are not just in the individual but also in the interconnections—the relationship system—with others."

It was time for me to take on the task of understanding how I was contributing to my depression, and to finally take responsibility for the part I was playing in my relationships. Doing this taught me that it's one thing to know something, but quite another to actually understand it—and something else altogether to apply it. Knowledge is only power if you continue to apply it and are mindful while doing so. As a client on her journey of making some difficult changes told me, "When starting to make a change to better your life and take responsibility for yourself it can seem like the hardest thing in the world to do, but once you do it a few times, it's the easiest thing. Because you create a habit that is better for you in the long run, but you have to actually do it for yourself first."

When you first start making yourself a top priority, you might feel self-centered and narcissistic, even if you're being honest with yourself about how you contribute to the issues in your relationships. After all, you aren't used to taking your feelings into account. But blaming others for their demands or your problems won't help your situation either. You're the only person who has control over your life, and with that control comes the power to make necessary changes. In order to feel free, you have to accept the challenge and work hard on building yourself so you can have a better future. You must shut the door on who you think you should be, and create the space for you to become who you want to be. This will leave you with more options for your life.

When you feel trapped and helpless, it can result in feelings of depression. As self-help writer Dr. Harriet B. Braiker says, "Whenever your thinking is contaminated by should, musts, oughts, and have to's, it is rigid, inflexible, and extreme. Rational thinking that will serve you better is flexible, moderate, and balanced." Knowing you have the power to alter your life gives you the confidence you need to take over your own choices.

Make Time for Yourself

If your identity and self-worth depend too much on your ability to do things for others, you're adding more stress to your life and the lives of everyone around you. That was surely true for me. I used to think having fun, relaxing, watching TV, napping, or doing any leisurely activity at all was a waste of time. However, I've come to learn that spending time on myself is essential for my health, well-being, and productivity. I used to do relaxing things just to say I did them and get them out of the way. Instead of enjoying those activities, I spent the time thinking of all the other things I should be doing. It wasn't relaxing at all!

You might think you have more value if you live by the motto *all work and no play*, believing that your discipline will somehow make you more worthy and desirable. I used to ignore my need for playtime and rest. I had no empathy for myself when I had a headache or neck pain; instead, I saw it as a weakness. When your worth is so tangled up in how much you can do for other people, you don't take time to rest when you feel sick. You feel bad, useless, or depressed when you can't function as intensely as you usually do. You don't see the importance of taking it easy and taking care of yourself.

I never used to give myself permission to take a day off or make time to rest. I want you to know that if you're going through a tough time, are tired, or just need some time to yourself, it's perfectly okay. By no means does it make you less lovable, worthy, or capable. It just means you're human! Being human can be a messy, difficult, confusing, and sometimes painful experience. You don't need to have all the answers. You don't need to perfectly complete everything all the time. Cut yourself some slack. You're not expected to be superhuman. If you aim for perfection, you'll never be satisfied, unless your definition of perfection changes. To be perfectly human is to take it easy, relax, make mistakes, and not expect to do everything and have all the answers. It means loving your imperfections and self-soothing instead of self-recriminating.

Let's think about this for a moment. Right now, you're alive. The actual probability of you having been born at all is about 1 in 400 trillion. Let that sink in for a minute: 1 in 400 trillion! You're a miracle. But I'll bet you've never thought about it that way. Most people haven't. That's some mind-blowing, life-altering information right there, isn't it? And that's just the estimated statistics on being born in the history of this planet; imagine what the statistics are for being alive in this very moment. That might just totally blow us out of the water. Even though the odds were against you being here, you're alive, right here and now. So, what are you going to do about it? Being the miracle you are, I'd assume you would, at least, have the ability to live the life you want. No one should have the power to take that from you. If you need a reason to change or the strength to do so, start by being grateful for your life and your free will. You can't be grateful if you aren't truly living for self. I'm sure you have a lot to be grateful for, but perhaps it gets hidden behind the challenges you face—concealed by your desire to please, over-function, and prove your value.

Many of us have trained ourselves to look at the bad and constantly complain about our lives. We don't give ourselves the option to recognize all the miracles taking place around us. That's especially the case when we haven't taken owner-ship of our lives. In order to make a change, you have to train yourself to look at the unique, enjoyable moments you've been overlooking—like the fact that you're alive and breathing! You have to remember how special and fortunate you are. When you know this to be true, you'll want to experience life for your self. You're unique, you deserve to be free and act for self. You have something to be grateful for—something to offer that goes far beyond pleasing other people. You have to believe that and honor yourself, your goals, and your dreams. Once you do that, your journey toward self-fullness will flow more naturally. You deserve to experience this life, with all your essence and authenticity, as the person you are and were meant to be. You're a miracle, so start acting like it.

Being Attuned to How Other People Feel

All her life, Claire had had a problem figuring out where other people ended and she began. All her life, she'd taken on the world's hurt; she held herself responsible. But why?

~ Elin Hilderbrand

Underneath all your people-pleasing ways, there's a sensitive person. I don't mean that you're the kind of person whose feelings are easily hurt. What I mean is that you're attuned to how other people feel; so when they hurt, you do, too. If you were ever spanked as a child, you might have heard your parent say, "This is going to hurt me more than it will hurt you." It can be challenging to let go of the idea that wanting to be more of a self will hurt the people we love. This idea still trips me up to do this day. But I know that if I don't keep it in check, I'll stay trapped trying to please others to avoid hurting their feelings. Your efforts to become more self-full might initially bother some people; however, you must learn how to manage your emotions around disappointing others. It will serve you well to do that instead of tirelessly trying to never disappoint people.

As I've said repeatedly, our ideas about what is truly beneficial for our relationships needs to be challenged. It isn't giving all of yourself and putting others first, thinking that makes you a good partner, friend, or member of society. It isn't blaming yourself for someone else's life decisions. It certainly isn't taking other people's feelings personally, considering them before you consider yourself. Blaming ourselves for other people's emotions narrows the truth by making only one party responsible for everything. In reality, all issues that occur in relationships are shared issues. The emotions that come from blaming yourself will keep you trapped in the cycle of trying to please other people. People-pleasers are driven by a belief that they'll be fulfilled by somehow taking away everyone's hurt. But if you're chasing the wrong objectives, you'll always wind up making things worse without knowing why. You aren't responsible for how other people feel about or react to your efforts to become a more self-full person. It's okay to be vulnerable, raw, and open about what you need; if other people are offended by that, it's okay. It's also okay to upset other people. They'll understand in time, and everyone will mature in the process.

Response Versus Reaction

When you set out to change, it's important to try respond-
ing to people rather than reacting emotionally to them.
Reacting once you've gotten fed up guarantees that when
you speak, you'll be doing so out of anger. And, of course,
anger makes us think and say crazy things. We actually believe
we make sense when, in reality, we're completely irrational.
Like a drunk person who doesn't know when it's time to
stop, anger hinders your judgment and makes you unaware
of what's happening.

When you're angry, you're under the influence of strong
chemicals. The amygdala, the part of your brain that initially
triggers anger, is one of the most primitive parts of the brain.
Once your amygdala alerts your body that you're angry, your
adrenal gland kicks into action. Adrenaline is a chemical that
increases your heart rate, forcing body contractions and blood
flow to your brain and muscles. Your body then starts produc-
ing more testosterone, a chemical that kicks your aggression
into higher gear. When your body reacts to your rage, it ramps
up the intensity by making you even more manic. This is why
anger makes you say and do crazy things that don't reflect the
truth of who you really are. Contrary to what people think,
anger doesn't make you speak the truth. It makes you speak
from the most primitive part of yourself. Basically, you'll
have a more rational conversation with a chimp who's high
on marijuana than you will with an angry person.

When people react to situations with anger, there's more
to the story. Behind their rage is a fear of being hurt, a fear
of not being able to stand up for themselves, or a fear of
unjust or unfair things happening. These are all reasonable
feelings. However, when those rational feelings are masked
by anger, the situation can intensify. That's because anger

tends to exaggerate the truth, making things worse than if they were responded to in a rational way.

I once worked with a client named Michael who worked hard at managing his anger and staying centered and grounded whenever he was challenged. Through much effort and practice, he learned to act differently and respond rationally to people under circumstances that used to provoke his anger. Eventually, Michael's world and relationships reflected what he really wanted, instead of what his anger wanted. Anger can dominate your thinking and infuse your life circumstances with anxiety, making it hard for you to see the facts. That's why it was important for Michael to take his time and see what emotions were lurking behind his anger. By practicing letting his emotions settle, Michael became capable of speaking up about what was bothering him.

When he was younger, Michael was taught to act out when he was upset. "Boys weren't promoted to talk things out but to work them out with their fists," Michael explained. He entered group therapy for anger management when he started to hit his children. He didn't want to repeat his father's mistakes, so he decided to get help changing his response to his children when he was angry. Through therapy, he learned new ways to manage himself when he was stressed. He started to become self-aware and made a commitment to find new, less destructive ways of managing his anxiety. That's the difference between reacting emotionally and responding logically to the people in your life. It's becoming aware of yourself, and not looking to immediately find relief. Your relationships are always a work in progress, but they'll become much more fulfilling as you learn how to better express yourself. Once Michael learned to clearly communicate the rules of the house to his children, he saw better results. Whenever one of his children broke a rule, he was able to respond without aggression. He was able to get upset while still keeping in mind that he loved his children and didn't want to do anything to affect their relationship. It's important to be able to stay emotionally connected to your loved ones even when you're upset with them. As Psychiatrist Murray Bowen explained, "It means being able to calmly reflect on a conflicted interaction afterward, realizing your own role in it, and then choosing a different response for the future." If you find yourself getting overly angry with your loved ones, you might benefit from taking these steps, which Michael took to respond differently to the people in his life.

1. Respond, don't react. Your immediate response is probably going to be anger; but if you've worked on being confident in yourself and your decisions, you'll have an easier time overcoming your desire to get angry and act out.

2. Create internal calm. Try to remain calm and centered, whether the metaphorical slap in the face comes from family, friends, or someone at work. Hurt feelings can fuel anger, because they bring up feelings of inadequacy. By all means, let yourself get angry. But be aware that most of the time, expressing that anger will only make matters worse and give the person you're angry with the high ground. No doubt it will prevent him or her from listening to you. So when the impulse to use harsh words or take reckless actions come, take a minute to breathe and get grounded. Then channel your logical brain and access the calm place within before responding.

3. Repeat the other person's words. Never pressure yourself to have the perfect response to another person. Instead, repeat the other person's words and/or actions, making sure you clearly understood. You can start by saying, "I want to be sure I heard you correctly," and then repeat the person's words how you heard them. The objective is to focus on the words themselves, not the emotions they provoke. Take the focus off your reaction and put it back onto the actual words or actions. This will help you stay clear and grounded in the facts, while also allowing you time to center yourself before responding.

4. Open up the discussion. Your loved ones might be surprised when they see that you're no longer overly emotional, which could allow them to think more deeply about their words and actions. Once this happens, a real discussion can take place. It's helpful to use language that shows your perspective. For example: "I can see how you might get that idea, but allow me to tell you my thoughts." This shows that you're open to seeing another perspective, disarming the other person and creating the potential for a productive dialogue. If you get defensive or disregard the other person's statements, you're less likely to be heard.

Human Connection

Life isn't much without human connection. In fact, we're biologically wired for relationships. Think about how boring and purposeless this life would be without friendships, intimate relationships, or family. Being human comes with a desire to be loved and accepted for who we are—and to offer the same to others. Did you know that newborn babies need to be held and embraced in order to experience healthy psychological development? Studies show that newborn babies with little to no human connection and comfort don't develop in healthy ways and, in some cases, even die.

Therefore, it's important to be aware of the consequences of isolating yourself or pulling away from people when you become overwhelmed or resentful. Remaining connected is learning to navigate the uncharted territory of being vulnerable in relationships. When we lose the ability to be vulnerable and close ourselves off to love, we also lose our ability to experience the joy that comes from relationships. As Brene Brown says, "We cannot selectively numb emotions; when we numb the painful emotions, we also numb the positive emotions."

Allowing yourself to be vulnerable requires you to be open to the parts of you that you closed off by engaging in pleasing behaviors. Vulnerability is hard to express, because it involves accessing parts of yourself that others may have disapproved of in the past. That's probably why you didn't access those parts of yourself to begin with. When you develop a strong sense of self, you'll learn to better manage your emotions when people are disapproving of you, because you'll be aware of and open to your vulnerabilities. Once you become aware of all the parts of yourself, you won't feel the need to close yourself off. When you deeply and solidly love yourself, your approval meter will be self-generated. It takes a lot of strength to honor all the parts of you, regardless of the opinions of others. Instead of avoiding the people in your life who don't always agree with you, face them. Not because you hatefully oppose them, but because you accept yourself and are comfortable with who you are, no matter how much they might disapprove of you.

My Results

Not in a million years did I think making my needs a priority, being vulnerable, and expressing what I needed from people would actually help my relationships flourish. But it all happened. I no longer see my family members as self-involved, needy people—and now I get love and support from them, too. When I started to account for what I needed, so did they. When my mother calls, she first asks me, "Is now a good time to talk?" She'll also say things like, "If what I'm saying upsets you, we don't have to talk about it." When my cousin calls me, she asks me how I'm doing and how my life is going. She used to never ask anything about me; she'd just go on talking about herself and what she needed. One day I told her, "You know, I only hear from you when something's wrong. I know that things are good when I don't hear from you. I'd love to hear about your life when things are going well for you. I'd also like it if you would ask every once in a while how I'm doing." She responded quite well to that. I think for a while she just got used to our relationship being a one-way street. Now she makes it a point to tell me the positives in her life and also ask me how I'm doing.

Many of my clients have explained how gaining awareness of themselves, changing their behaviors, and building a self with personal values has benefitted them. It wasn't easy for most of them, and sometimes they still face obstacles that stump them. I do, too. We've all put work into looking at our natural responses and deciding to either fall into old patterns or find the confidence within ourselves to act in ways that better align with our values. Instead of shutting out the facts of our circumstances and moving forward, we seek ways to draw upon our internal strength and respond thoughtfully to situations, rather than react in ways that showcase our insecurities.

Don't Expect to Always Get It Right

Don't expect to be happy all the time, and try not to judge yourself when you aren't. I used to judge myself for feeling down, then judge myself for judging myself. There was a time when I thought I had to rise above my emotions. I believed I had to avoid feeling depressed, lonely, defeated, or sad and only concentrate on good emotions. But I've learned that a big part of being self-full is leaving room for all emotions, knowing they're all part of the growth process.

In the beginning, I went too far in the opposite direction and pulled away from the people in my life. I left everyone who relied on me hanging, because I didn't know how to be present with them without losing myself. You can still be there for people, and your loved ones will still need you from time to time. However, being there for people doesn't mean rescuing them. All you can do is be present with your empathy. My husband once asked me, "Why, when an issue comes up, do you think you have to be the one to solve it? You put that pressure on yourself." He was right. Whenever something came up, I'd get anxious because I'd put the weight on myself to fix the problem. It's freeing to be able to get curious and be present, without feeling the need to fix or rescue.

In the beginning of my transition, I was so frustrated and annoyed with the people in my life that I left them high and dry. Looking back, I see I pulled away too much and too fast. I was backing out of my driveway, pushing hard on the gas, without looking at my backup camera. I did this because I didn't want to deal with the pressure I thought others were putting on me. I was fed up, so I didn't care who or what was behind me. Later I realized I was the one responsible for putting the pressure on myself. No one was purposely sucking my life energy out of me. They didn't know how they were affecting me; and since I always jumped in to take over, they didn't trust themselves to solve their own conflicts.

For the most part, I don't believe people do things with ill intentions. Sometimes they just don't know how their actions come across. That's why communication is so important and why working toward self-fullness is invaluable. You can't just make a run for it, put the peddle to the metal, and never look back. Eventually, you'll hit a wall. Once you start to understand people in their context and allow them to see where you're coming from, your relationships will become a reciprocal, mutually shared, give-and-take process. They'll become enjoyable instead of draining. That's because you'll be coming from a place of understanding instead of resentment and anger.

Conclusion

> *Your time is limited, so don't waste it living someone else's life. Don't be trapped by dogma-which is living with the results of other people's thinking. Don't let the noise of other people's opinions drown your own inner voice. And most important, have the courage to follow your heart and intuition. They somehow know what you truly want to become. Everything else is secondary.*
>
> ~ STEVE JOBS

Being a dedicated people-pleaser led me to forget about my needs, as I'm sure it's done for you. My mission to build myself has proven difficult at times, but it's been a necessary and transformative process of development. It included looking at myself honestly and seeing how I contributed to my issues as well as other people's struggles. I was lost for quite some time, endlessly aiming to please the people in my life. I had the American Dream, but because I wasn't being true to myself, it felt more like a nightmare. I thought I was supposed to be the perfect family member—the one who always had her life together—but I was missing something vitally important: myself.

I wrote this book to share with you my relentless quest to discover my purpose and create a self. Once I created self-fullness in my life, I knew I wanted to tell my story—mostly in hopes that it could assist other people in changing theirs. In part, I also wrote this book to help myself as I continue along my personal journey. I've made changes that I never would have thought possible for my life. The same is possible for you, too. Remember that progress happens slowly. Patience! Agency, competency, maturity, and autonomy shall be yours.

Figuring out who you want to be is an ever-evolving process. But it starts now! Now is the time to start taking yourself on—and remember, all changes start with awareness. As I've stressed throughout the book, an instrumental part of creating a life worth living is developing a self-full mindset, because the way you perceive things is a fundamental and unavoidable part of your reality. You must first change your mindset and perceptions before you can make any meaningful behavioral changes. When you develop a self-full mindset, you become aware that you're doing what's best for you and for other people at the same time. That's why self-fullness isn't selfishness.

The self-full process is about trial and error. It's about making mistakes, changing your behaviors, and making your own decisions. I started to develop confidence when I decided to think for myself and move forward with my decisions. Life is more exciting once you learn to stop taking responsibility for everyone else's life and start living for yourself. If you don't learn to let go, you'll keep trying to control the situations and people around you. A big part of letting go is getting comfortable with the unknown and realizing you really don't have control over other people's lives anyway. If you want real control, lose the illusion of control. You do this by putting effort into becoming self-full, making ongoing efforts to be mindful of the ways you respond to others. When you accept who you are and place less judgment on yourself, you'll no longer need other people to feel worthy; you'll be able to give that sense of worthiness to yourself.

Let go of the idea that people need saving, and that it's your responsibility to do it. Somewhere down the road, you internalized the message that you had to be responsible for how others feel. But the truth is, you aren't responsible for anyone else's feelings but your own. It's okay to upset people, disagree, and ruffle some feathers, as long as you're acting for self. Remember that you can feel for other people without taking over for them, especially when doing so undercuts their functioning. You can't live a healthy, fulfilled, happy life if you're too busy managing your feelings and other people's feelings at the same time. Remember, people can take care of themselves. Most importantly, you can manage your discomfort around other people's disappointment.

One Foot Off the Ledge

I'll leave you with this story. I was waiting for one of my clients, Sam, to arrive one Friday morning and started to get concerned. It was a few minutes after our session time, and he was never one to arrive late. I had a sinking feeling that something was terribly wrong. Sam was an attractive, wealthy male client in his mid-20s who'd first started coming to me a few months earlier to work on what he described as "feeling lost." He explained to me that he was brought up with financial stability and had built his own successful investment company. He told me he constantly had conflicting viewpoints about things and felt nothing was ever good enough for him; he always wanted more. He also had a tough time in relationships, because he always wanted his girlfriends to have everything and would do whatever it took to make them happy. When his most recent girlfriend broke up with him, he started feeling suicidal. He couldn't deal with the pain of rejection, because he'd based his self-worth on what other people thought of him. He explained that he loved his girlfriend very much and had done whatever she wanted to keep her, but that it only resulted in the opposite of what he wanted. He ended up pushing her away by acting needy.

That particular girl wasn't after him for his money, and she had a hard time being with someone who never felt satisfied. She felt pressured to complete parts of Sam he wasn't completing for himself. Even the love she offered was never enough. That's because Sam wasn't giving himself the love and recognition he was striving to give to others. He was the only one who could fill that void, but he didn't realize it. He kept thinking that if only he could make more money in the market, meet more women, and buy more material things, he'd finally feel fulfilled and worthy.

Sam had never been rejected before, so he was having a particularly tough time with his most recent breakup. If you base your self-worth on others' acceptance of you, rejection is the ultimate betrayal. When Sam didn't show up for our usual scheduled appointment, I knew something was terribly wrong. I called his cell phone, but it went straight to voicemail. With no hesitation, I called the local police department.

I explained that I had a suicidal client who didn't show up for a session and that they needed to check on him at his residence immediately.

When the police got to Sam's condo, they called me saying he wasn't answering the door, but the doorman hadn't seen him leave. I said, "Break in the door or get a key from the front desk quickly." I must say, I'm not an impulsive or reactive person, but everything inside me knew they had to get in that condo, and fast. The next thing I heard the police officer say was, "There's someone on the ledge of their balcony." Then suddenly, my cell phone lost connection. I started pacing back and forth, biting my nails and praying that Sam was okay. I knew he was suicidal, so I had done everything I could to ensure his safety.

After what seemed like an eternity, my phone finally rang, and it was the officer. I picked up without hesitation. "Okay," the officer said, "We have him sedated. We had to wrestle him to the ground. He had one foot off the ledge when we got to him. He was about to jump." I started breathing again. As sad as I felt for Sam, I felt even more relieved that he hadn't taken his life. I use his story as a reminder of how important it is to aim for self-fullness. He was so down that he wanted to kill himself because his entire sense of self-worth was rooted in what other people thought of him. His emotions fluctuated like stock market prices, and he never felt content.

If I didn't change, I could have been right where Sam was: hopeless, depressed, unfulfilled, and needy for love. It's a terrible place to be. After some time, Sam and I rebuilt our therapeutic relationship. At first, he was angry with me for calling the police, because he didn't want to live. But after some time, he forgave me. He said, "Looking down from my balcony knowing I was going to die changed something in me. It was like a surrender of control. That was it, all I had to do was let go and it would be over."

Death is the ultimate transition. When facing it, Sam was strengthened to make the necessary changes in his life. Despite all his cars, travels, women, and money, Sam was missing the most important thing: a sense of self. He didn't have anyone he could count on. After some time, though, he learned to be attuned to himself and mindful about what he wanted, without judging himself for it. Finally, *he* became the person he could count on. After our sessions, I'd write Sam letters summarizing our time together. I'll leave you with one of those letters.

Dear Sam,

   Thus far we've symbolically traveled into the uncharted territory of your life and experiences. It seems that being lost has allowed you to travel to a new land and take different routes in your life that may not have been predicted by your original story. Sometimes we need to be lost and lonely before we find our way to the places we really want to be in this life. Going through this journey with society, the good, the immature, the confident, the judgmental, the analytical, the greedy, the interpreter, the philosopher, and the positive voices following you and pulling you in different directions, how is it that you'll find your own voice? It's hard to know what you prefer in this life or have a sense of where you're going with all that chatter going on; it may even blur your vision a little bit on your way. It's also difficult to know ourselves in the midst of interactions with others that may tell a contrary story to what we know about ourselves. On your journey, you may find out things you never knew about yourself. Some things you may like (for example, when you help out a friend), and others you may not like (for example, lying about your age). You may even notice on your journey that you won't know the consequences of your actions until after the fact, and only then you can look back and mark the spots on your map to know what direction you might take the next time. The map you use to find your way may seem clear, but as you follow it, you may notice things happening that the map could never have predicted. The journey would be so much easier if there was just one way to get to where you're going and if you knew all the stops. But how much fun would that be? It would be like going to Paris with a plan, instead of in the spur of the moment. Sometimes it's great to have all the answers and know exactly where you're heading; but other times you need to get a little lost to learn and to grow into the person you prefer to be. That's a journey that never ends but has interesting stops and bumps along the road. As a Buddhist philosopher once said, "Life is a great mystery to be lived moment by moment, not a problem to be solved once and for all." I will ask you to take with you what you want from our time together, and to leave behind what does not fit with you.

Talk soon,

Dr. Ilene

BIBLIOGRAPHY

Agrov, S. (2002). *Why Men Love Bitches: From Doormat to Dreamgirl: A Woman's Guide to Holding Her Own in a Relationship.* Adams Media, Massachusetts.

Bateson, G. (2000). *Steps to an Ecology of Mind: Collected Essays in Anthropology, Psychiatry, Evolution, and Epistemology.* The University of Chicago Press, Chicago.

Beaugard, M. and O'Leary, D. (2008). *The Spiritual Brain: A Neuroscientist's Case for the Existence of the Soul.* HarperCollins, New York.

Bertolino, B. and O' Hanlon, B. (2002). *Even from a Broken Web: Brief, Respectful Solution-Oriented Therapy for Sexual Abuse and Trauma.* W. W. Norton & Company, New York.

Bowen, M. (1978). *Family Therapy in Clinical Practice.* Jason Aronson, New York.

Braiker, H.B. (2001). *The Disease to Please: Curing the People-Pleasing Syndrome.* McGraw-Hill, New York.

Brown, B. (2010). *The Gifts of Imperfection: Let Go of Who You Think You're Supposed to Be and Embrace Who You Are.* Hazelden, Minnesota.

Brown, J. (2012). *Growing Yourself Up: How to Bring Your Best to All of Life's Relationships.* Exisle, New Zealand.

Bucay, J. (2005). *The Power of Self-Dependence: Allowing Yourself to Live Life on Your Own Terms*. Harper Paperbacks, New York.

Chodron, P. (2016). *When Things Fall Apart: Heart Advice for Difficult Time*. Shambhala Publications, Colorado.

Dyer, W.W. 1976, *Your Erroneous Zones: Bold but Simple Techniques for Taking Charge of Your Unhealthy Behavior Patterns*. Funk & Wagnalls, New York.

Gilbert, R. (1999). *Extraordinary Relationships: A New Way of Thinking About Human Interactions*. John Wiley, New York.

Hoff, B. (1982). *The Tao of Pooh*. Penguin Book, New York.

Jackson, P. (2006). *Sacred Hoops: Spiritual Lessons of a Hardwood Warrior*. Hachette Books, New York.

Jung, C. (1955). *Modern Man in Search of a Soul*. Houghton Mifflin Harcourt Publishing Company, New York.

Kerr, M.E. and Bowen, M. (1988). *Family Evaluation: An Approach Based on Bowen Theory*. Norton, New York.

Kersey, C. (1998). *Unstoppable: 45 Powerful Stories of Perseverance and Triumph from People Just Like You*. Source Books, Illinois.

Lewis, T., Amini, F. and Lannon, R. (2001). *A General Theory of Love*. Random House, New York.

Myss, C. (2003). *Sacred Contracts: Awakening Your Divine Potential*. Three Rivers Press, New York.

Noone, R.J. and Papero, D.V. (2015). *The Family Emotional System: An Integrative Concept for Theory, Science, and Practice.* Lexington Books, Maryland.

Schwartz, J.M. and Begley, S. (2003). *The Mind & The Brain: Neuroplasticity and the Power of Mental Force.* ReganBooks, New York.

Shnarch, D. (1997). *Passionate Marriage: Love, Sex, and Intimacy in Emotionally Committed Relationships.* Norton, New York.

Strayed, C. (2015). *Brave Enough.* Alfred A. Knopf, Canada.

Titelman, P. (Ed.) (2008). *Triangles: Bowen Family Systems Theory Perspectives.* Haworth Clinical Practice Press, New York.

Walsch, N.D. (1995). *Conversations with God: An Uncommon Dialogue.* Berkley Books, New York.

Weakland, J.H. and Wendel, A.R. (2014). *Propagations: Thirty Years of Influence from the Mental Research Institute.* Routledge, London.

INDEX

ACKNOWLEDGMENTS

THIS IS THE FIRST BOOK I'VE EVER WRITTEN. Well, if you count my dissertation, it's the second book I've ever written. But I hope this one is more than just a research project. I hope it's the kind of book that serves to change lives other than my own. I never thought I could actually do something like this. I spent lots of time wondering if all my hard work would even be worth it. But to my surprise I stuck to the process, and now I find myself proud of the end result, knowing I couldn't have done it alone. Some people gave me inspiration through their narratives, others pushed me by believing in my abilities, and those who changed through our work together gave me the faith I needed to tell their stories. I owe so many people so much—far beyond what I can put into words. Since I've been talking about this book for almost two years now, I just want to say that I appreciate, with all my heart, every last one of you. Thank you for your unique contributions, and for the lessons I never would have learned without you.

Denise Fournier, editing genius, you know what I want to say and help me express it in words that will make more sense to my readers. You've given me that extra push to see that I could put my ideas into writing, and you've helped me stay on course throughout this process.

Edrica Richardson, you read through my entire book draft when I wasn't sure about it, and you lifted me up with your kind words and enthusiasm. I'm grateful for the great friend and colleague you've been to me.

Jim Rudes, without our time in therapy together, I'd probably be a very different person than who I am today. You helped me see things in a new way, and the perspective I gained through our work together changed my life.

Olivia S. Colmer, you've always been a positive force in my life, inviting me to join you on an intensive Bowen training journey that opened my eyes. You've been a wonderful colleague and friend.

Corinne Dannon, my most creative and humble friend, you've always been encouraging and a great person to go to for ideas.

Shirley Bronstein, you've been my best friend and soul sister for many years. You've always been there for me, listening to me talk about this book over and over again, and believing in me when I didn't believe in myself.

Jaime Wasser, you've listened to my ideas and helped me change some aspects of this book to make it better. I appreciate all the support you've given me.

Michelle Dempsey, though you came into the picture later in the process, your insight and drive have been instrumental in helping me see this book through.

Greg and Dina Dunkley, you've been with me since the beginning of my blog, and you've helped me get my career to where it is today. I can never repay you for all of the support you've given me.

To my Bowen training group, meeting with you all those Saturdays meant a lot to me. I learned so much from all of you, and I never could have created this book without you.

There's no way to overstate the contribution my clients have made to this book. I'm astonished every day by your strength and resilience. Thank you for opening up to me, and for letting me share your stories so that others can learn from your example and improve their lives.

Moises Cohen, we've known each other our entire lives. You've witnessed my transition the most, and you've always been supportive when it comes to my needs. You've helped me flourish and, like you would say, grow a stronger backbone.

Emily, my baby, I hope I help nourish your sense of self as you get older. I'm proud of the little lady you've become, and I'll always love you.

To my in-laws, who are so very special to me, I'm happy we joined our families together; I've learned so much from all of you.

To my siblings and cousins, thank you for letting me share our story. You all mean the world to me.

Dad, thanks for always pushing me to be better and do better.

Mom, I think you've been the most supportive of all. I see not only my evolution in this process, but yours, too.

Thank you all for being who you are and contributing what you have to this book and to my life.

IN LOVING MEMORY OF
FRED S. STRAUSS

Grandpa, you're my inspiration and the reason I've done what I have for our family and for myself. Memories of you keep me grounded, grateful, and humble. You'll forever be missed.

ILENE S. COHEN

"Dr. Ilene" S. Cohen, Ph.D., is a psychotherapist and blogger, who teaches in the Department of Counseling at Barry University. She's a regular contributor to *Psychology Today*, and her work has appeared in Psych Central and Tiny Buddha. Both her book and practice are fueled by her passion for helping people achieve their goals, build a strong sense of self, and lead fulfilling and meaningful lives. As a president of her family's foundation, she oversees myriad initiatives geared towards creating better opportunities for those in need.

To contact Dr. Ilene you can visit her website at:
www.doctorilene.com.

Made in the USA
Lexington, KY
11 February 2018